A Sweet Exposition on Psalm 23

and

An Exhortation to the Carrying of Christ's Cross

This volume contains facsimiles of the 1846 Parker Society modern-spelling editions of Myles Coverdale's 16th century works:

A SWEET EXPOSITION ON PSALM 23

originally entitled
A VERY EXCELLENT AND SWETE EXPOSITION UPON THE TWO AND TWENTYE PSALME OF DAVID

AND

AN EXHORTATION TO THE CARRYING OF CHRIST'S CROSS

originally entitled
AN EXHORTATION TO THE CARIENGE OF CHRYSTES CROSSE WITH A TRUE AND BREFE CONFUTATION OF FALSE AND PAPISTICALL DOCTRYNE

WITH ALSO

an appendix by Ruth Magnusson Davis
KEEP THEE UNTO THE WORD

THE MISSION of Baruch House Publishing, founded by editor Ruth Magnusson (Davis), is to bring to the world again the lost works of the early English Reformation. Our main focus is the 1537 Matthew Bible, and our ongoing work is to gently update it for readers today, with reference to the editor's own 1549 edition of the Matthew Bible. The Matthew Bible was the joint work of William Tyndale (c.1491-1536), Myles Coverdale (c.1487-1569), and John Rogers (c.1500-1555). It is the only English Bible that was bought with blood: both Tyndale and Rogers were burned at the stake for their work.

Baruch House has also undertaken to re-publish individually the best of Myles Coverdale's treatises and small books in an attractive, easy-to-read format, including to date:

Hope of the Faithful. A defence of the traditional doctrine of heaven and hell. An appendix shows how the change from "hell" to "Sheol" and "Hades" in the 1894 Revised Version of the Bible defeated the traditional doctrine.

Fruitful Lessons. Upbuilding teaching and instruction on the Passion, Death, Resurrection and Ascension of Christ, and of the sending of the Holy Spirit.

Treatise on Death. Deep and profound teachings on how to prepare for our own death, deal with those who are dying, and comfort the bereaved.

A Sweet Exposition on Psalm 23. Restoring the lost teaching that in Psalm 23 David was praising the word of God as the pasture and refreshing drink of God's sheep and the table set before them in the presence of their enemies.

OTHER PUBLICATIONS of Baruch House include:

The October Testament. The New Testament of the New Matthew Bible (NMB), published in 2016.

The Story of the Matthew Bible: Part 1, That Which We First Received. The full, true, and neglected story of the making of the Matthew Bible.

The Story of the Matthew Bible: Part 2, The Scriptures Then and Now. Part 2 tracks the often-startling changes made to the original Bible translations of William Tyndale and Myles Coverdale after the Reformation and examines the motivations behind some of them.

More information is on our websites:
www.baruchhousepublishing.com
www.newmatthewbible.org

EXPOSITION UPON THE TWENTY-SECOND PSALM
&
EXHORTATION TO THE CARRYING OF CHRIST'S CROSS
by Bishop Myles Coverdale. This edition 1846.

From *Remains of Myles Coverdale,*
published by the Parker Society.

The Society was "Instituted A.D. M.DCCC.XL for the publication of the Works of the Fathers and Early Writers of the Reformed English Church."

EDITED FOR

𝕮𝖍𝖊 𝓟𝖆𝖗𝖐𝖊𝖗 𝓢𝖔𝖈𝖎𝖊𝖙𝖞,

BY THE

REV. GEORGE PEARSON, B.D.

RECTOR OF CASTLE CAMPS,

AND LATE CHRISTIAN ADVOCATE IN THE UNIVERSITY OF CAMBRIDGE.

CAMBRIDGE:
PRINTED AT
THE UNIVERSITY PRESS.

M.DCCC.XLVI.

Copyright © 2022 Ruth Magnusson Davis (Baruch House Publishing)

The facsimiles of "A very excellent and swete exposition upon the two and twentye psalme of David" and "An exhortation to the carienge of Chrystes crosse with a true and brefe confutation of false and papisticall doctrine" are taken with gratitude from the Parker Society modern-spelling collection *Remains of Myles Coverdale*, published in 1846. The originals are in the public domain; however, a considerable amount of work has been invested in preparation of the facsimile for this edition. All rights are reserved. No part of this publication may be reproduced, stored in a retrieval system, or transmitted, in any form or by any means, electronic, mechanical, photocopying, recording, or otherwise, without the prior permission of the publisher.

Contact publisher through the website at **www.baruchhousepublishing.com**.

Scripture quotations are from The October Testament, the New Testament of the New Matthew Bible (NMB) and the 1537/49 Matthew Bible. Quotations from other Bibles are used only for the purpose of comment, criticism, and education about the history of Bible revision since the Reformation.

Cover design by Iryna Spica

ISBNs
Paperback 978-1-7771987-8-7
Hardcover 978-1-7771987-9-4

About the cover
The beautiful mosaic pictured on the cover, made by an unknown artist, sits above the entrance to the Mausoleum of Galla Placidia in Ravenna, Italy. Called "The Good Shepherd," it dates back to about 425 AD. Jesus Christ is the heavenly shepherd, and his staff is a cross, symbolizing how he purchased his sheep. Altogether there are six sheep with him, which is half the apostolic number and is believed to symbolize the flock of the faithful. He is seated in a pasture where he tends his sheep, and is shown reaching over to comfort one of them.

Table of Contents

Publisher's Foreword ... xi

A Sweet Exposition on Psalm 23
by Myles Coverdale ... 19

An Exhortation to the
Carrying of Christ's Cross
by Myles Coverdale ... 59

Appendix
Keep Thee unto the Word
by Ruth Magnusson Davis ... 113

Glossary
Early Modern English Words ... 213

Publisher's Foreword

THIS BOOK IS the fourth volume in the Baruch House series featuring the best works of Myles Coverdale, works that have been lost to the world for centuries.

It is an unfortunate twist of history that God's servant Myles Coverdale (c1488-1569), who was one of the most productive and effective of the English Reformers, is one of the least known and least acknowledged. He almost single-handedly gave us his 1535 Bible, which was the world's first printed English Bible and the first to be licensed for use in the Church. From this great work he also contributed over half of the Old Testament Scriptures and the Apocryphal books of the 1537 Matthew Bible, and then he was the chief editor of the Great Bible, first published in 1539. He is the only man to have so greatly contributed to all three of England's Reformation Bibles. These precious gifts to his country were in addition to his translations of selected works of the European Reformers, his own writings, and his labours for the English Church, in which he was ordained a bishop.

This volume contains two of Coverdale's great faith-building treatises, though they were published during very different times for the faith in England. The first is *A very excellent and swete exposition upon the two and twentye Psalme of David*, which we have retitled *A Sweet Exposition on Psalm 23*. (See the Appendix for information about the numbering of the psalms.)

Coverdale published this treatise at the beginning of the Reformation in England, a hopeful time when the light of God's word had just begun to shine in that country.

However, the second treatise, his *Exhortation to the Carrying of Christ's Cross,* was published shortly after Mary Tudor, the tragic Roman Catholic queen, had ascended the throne and begun her work of snuffing out the light. Thus these treatises form bookends to the English Reformation. They take us from a time of blossoming hope to a time when, to all appearances, hope had been crushed. Yet they both confidently proclaim the unseen and eternal hope: the faith which never perishes, and which no man nor evil time can take away, so long as the smouldering wick remains.

The Sweet Exposition on Psalm 23

In 1537, the year following his return to England after a long exile in Europe, where he had fled for refuge from persecution, Coverdale published the treatise on Psalm 23. Important reforms were now underway under King Henry VIII's chief ministers Thomas Cromwell and Thomas Cranmer, and England was a safer place for Protestants. Thanks to Cromwell, Coverdale's 1535 Bible had recently been licensed for the Church; his remarkably clear translations, made mostly from the new German Bibles and therefore revealing Martin Luther's influence, were among the choicest firstfruits of the English Reformation. Since Coverdale also translated his *Sweet Exposition on Psalm 23* from Luther, it too reveals that man's influence; in particular, it reveals his great love and reverence for God's word, which Coverdale shared.

Given its original authorship, when we read the first person in the *Sweet Exposition,* we are reading the thoughts of

PUBLISHER'S FOREWORD

Martin Luther – as, for example, where he wrote about his battles for truth. He said he overcame his troubles and his enemies simply by resorting to the table of God's word; its truth, promises, and guidance were the only "harness," or armour and weaponry, in which he trusted. Every Christian should do likewise, he wrote, "and so shall he doubtless receive strength and comfort against everything that oppresseth him" (pp.51-54).

The *Sweet Exposition* sets forth the lost understanding that Psalm 23, also called the Shepherd's Psalm, was written in praise of the holy word of God. It is to restore this understanding – which truly is sweet to build faith and trust in God – that Baruch House has undertaken to republish Coverdale's treatise. In it we learn that David penned Psalm 23 in praise of God's word as the pasture where God's sheep find their goodly green grass and refreshing draughts of water. The word is also the table set before them in the presence of their enemies – "in the similitude," we learn, "of the table whereupon the shewbread lay continually." In some contexts, the sacraments of the word – baptism and the Lord's Supper – are in view. This treatise highlights the Reformers' great hope for the Church to be a true heavenly pasture and table, where God's word and sacraments would nourish, comfort, and refresh.

A thing to bear in mind when we read in the *Sweet Exposition* about the word of God being preached in the Church is that, in the early Lutheran and Anglican churches, this preaching was in large part given through liturgy, mostly composed of the pure words of Scripture with ancient common prayers, and through readings taken directly from the Bible. The readings were selected according to the days and seasons of the Christian calendar. Since many people did not have personal Bibles, they needed to go to church to hear the word. This explains the comments in the *Exposition* about how people starved for want of it when forced to live under hostile regimes where Christianity was suppressed, as under the Turks, or where it was falsely taught, as in the Roman Church. As well, the celebration of Holy Communion and Eucharistic remembrance of Christ was a central focus in the Reformation churches. Private sermons did not dominate like they often do now. In the Church of England, efforts were made to curtail "liberty of prophesying" in order to protect the sheep from the unwholesome pasture of men's opinions. Archbishop Cranmer would not even allow hymns, due to the risk of introducing man's doctrine. For many years, only the psalms were sung in the English Church, drawn from Coverdale's Psalter in the Great Bible. The goal was to keep the word of God pure and unadulterated in the congregations.

From light to darkness

After many labours, the English Reformers' hope for their Church appeared to have been fully realized – indeed, was realized – by 1553, sixteen years after Coverdale published his *Sweet Exposition* and just before Mary ascended the throne. Cranmer had completed massive reforms in the Church of England. Churchgoers enjoyed vernacular services following his Book of Common Prayer along with English Bible readings. He had compiled the holy liturgy from ancient sources, purged of medieval accretions and utilizing sentences and verses from the new English Scriptures. Excellent homilies were prescribed for common reading, so every congregation in the country could consistently receive the same profitable preaching. Finally, in 1553, the Articles of Religion were formulated, which established sound doctrine. The English Church was thus made a heavenly pasture indeed.

But all rejoicing over these accomplishments was extinguished when Mary was crowned queen in July that same year. She cast the English Bibles out of the Church along with all Cranmer's reforms, the Prayer Book, and the Articles, and set about to re-establish Roman Catholicism. She also renewed persecutions against the Protestants: her infamous and deadly persecutions earned her the epithet Bloody Queen Mary. With her advent came the fulfilment of Luther's observation in the *Exposition on Psalm 23* that, "as soon as the word of God goeth forth, and as soon as there be any that receive it and abide by it, immediately the devil and all his angels step forth, and move the world with all the power thereof against it to put it down, and utterly to destroy them that have it and acknowledge it." And though the circumstances differed, in another writing Luther complained of a similar phenomenon in Germany, where, he said, the true blessings of the gospel prevailed no longer than about twenty years.[1]

The Exhortation to the Carrying of Christ's Cross

In 1554, early in the dark reign of Queen Mary, Coverdale wrote the second treatise in this volume, *An Exhortation to the Carrying of Christ's Cross*. The Parker Society notice at the beginning of the work says it was published anonymously, but the internal and external evidence indicates Coverdale was the author. Given this, when we read the first person here, Coverdale is speaking for himself. In his opening remarks, he noted that things were bad in England and likely to get worse. At that

---

[1] Martin Luther, "Lectures on Genesis," Volume 4, *Luther's Works,* American Edition (Saint Louis: Concordia Publishing House, 1964), 213-14.

time his friend John Rogers, co-labourer with him for the English Bible and the compiler of the Matthew Bible, was imprisoned in Newgate, while Coverdale himself was under a form of house arrest. It was only through the intervention of the king of Denmark that Coverdale was eventually able to flee England and find refuge in Europe again, but Rogers went to death by burning in early 1555.

It is curious that Coverdale found means to publish his *Exhortation* in the oppressive climate that prevailed under Mary. It must have been printed on a secret press, or perhaps overseas, as his Bible had been almost twenty years before. One wonders how successfully it was distributed among the people.

What is striking about the *Exhortation*, and what makes it uniquely powerful, is its pure scriptural content. All Coverdale's years of labour with the English Bible bore hundredfold fruit in this treatise. The words and concepts of Scripture flowed naturally from his pen, and he wove Bible verses and stories together seamlessly to show why persecution is nothing strange, trouble cannot hurt God's children, and even that the cross is profitable to be borne. He then moved on and, with powerful and able arguments, refuted four contentious tenets of medieval papal doctrine – transubstantiation, the mass as a sacrifice, praying and sacrificing for the dead, and praying to the dead – and showed how they deny Christ's work and victory on the cross.

Coverdale urged believers to be steadfast in persecutions. He feared that, when threatened with prison, loss of goods, or death, they would be tempted to forswear the truth. He therefore wrote to set the truth clearly before their eyes and to exhort them to abide by it – to take up their cross, follow in the footsteps of Jesus, and look to the things that are eternal. In emphasizing this transcendent vision his *Exhortation* echoes the *Sweet Exposition,* where it was written that a sure and constant faith turns her back upon everything that is temporal and transitory. This vision is common to both treatises, though they were published in very different circumstances, because the common faith and eternal hope are independent of circumstance.

R.M.D.

This facsimile book has been carefully prepared from a publication that is now almost 180 years old. As with all our facsimile publications, Baruch House guarantees that there are no missing pages, and each page has received special attention to correct imperfections arising from age, damage, or the scanning process. As well, in this edition only we have in a few places, where possible, painstakingly and imperceptibly updated obsolete English words, such as "alway" to "always," "knowledge" to "acknowledge," etc. This will make for a clearer message and better reading experience.

The table of contents for *An Exhortation to the Carrying of Christ's Cross* was originally set at the end of that treatise. For the reader's convenience, we have moved it to the beginning of the treatise as a dedicated table, and manually renumbered the pages to accord with this edition. The *Exposition on Psalm 23* had no table of contents, but it follows the psalm logically and is short enough that it does not need one.

EXPOSITION

UPON THE

TWENTY-SECOND PSALM.

UPON THE TWENTY-SECOND PSALM.

The effect of this psalm. IN this psalm doth David and every christian heart give thanks and praise unto God for his most principal benefit, namely, for the preaching of his dear and holy word, whereby we are called, accepted, and numbered among the multitude, which is the congregation or church of God; where only, and in no place else, the pure doctrine, the true knowledge of God's will, and the right service of God is found and had.

But this same noble treasure doth holy David praise and extol marvellous excellently, with goodly, sweet, fair, and pure words, yea, and that with likenesses borrowed out of God's service of the old Testament.

A sheep. First, he likeneth himself to a sheep, whom God himself, as a faithful diligent shepherd, doth wondrous well take heed unto, feedeth him in a pleasant green pasture, which standeth full of good thick grass; where there is abundance also of fresh water, and no scarceness. *The shepherd.* Item, he likeneth God also unto such a shepherd, as with his staff leadeth and bringeth the sheep the plain right way, that it cannot go amiss, and defendeth his flock so with the sheep-hook, that the wolf cannot break in. *A guest.* After this doth he make himself a guest, for whom God prepareth a table, where he findeth both strength and comfort, refreshing and joy, and that plenteously.

The word of God hath many names. And thus the prophet giveth the word of God divers names, calleth it goodly pleasant green grass, fresh water, the right way, a staff, a sheep-hook, a table, balm, or pleasant oil, and a cup that is alway full. And this he doth not without a cause: for the power of God's word is manifold. For why? Like as a sheep in a fair pleasant meadow, beside the green grass and fresh water, in the presence of his shepherd which leadeth it with the staff or rod, so that it cannot go astray, and defendeth it so with the sheep-hook, that no harm can happen unto it, hath his food and pleasure in all safeguard; or like as a man lacketh nothing that sitteth at a table, where there is plenty of meat and drink, and all manner of comfort and gladness: so much more they that be the sheep of this shepherd, whereof this psalm singeth, lack no good thing, are richly provided for, not only in soul, but also in body; as Christ saith in the sixth of Matthew: " Seek first the kingdom of God and the righteousness thereof; so shall all these things be ministered unto you." For as they that want bodily food live in great straitness and pensiveness, not being able to fulfil the body's request in this behalf; even so also those that want this wholesome and necessary word of God, cannot rejoice nor be pacified inwardly. Yea, even as bread and wine refresh a man's fleshly heart, and make him joyful; even so the word of God quickeneth and refresheth a man's soul inwardly.

For when the word of God is truly and sincerely preached, look how many divers names the prophet giveth it here, so many commodities and fruits doth it bring. Unto them that are diligent and earnest to hear it, whom our Lord God knoweth only for his own sheep, it is a pleasant green grass, a fresh water, wherewith they are satisfied and refreshed. It keepeth them also in the right way, and preserveth them, that no misfortune nor harm happen unto them. Moreover, it is unto them a continual wealth, where there is abundance of meat and drink, and all manner of joy and pleasure: that is, they are not only instruct and guided, refreshed, strengthened, and comforted by the word of God, but ever more and more preserved in the right way, defended in all manner of trouble both of body and soul. And finally they have the victory, and prevail against all temptations and troubles, whereof they must abide right many, as the fourth verse doth specify. Shortly, they live in all manner of safeguard, as they unto whom no misfortune can happen, forasmuch as their shepherd doth feed them and preserve them. *The preaching of God's word bringeth prosperity.*

Therefore should we take instruction out of this psalm, not to despise the word of God, but gladly to hear and learn the same, to love it, and to make much of it, and to resort unto the little flock where we may have it; and again, on the other side, to flee and eschew those that do blaspheme and persecute it: for where this blessed light doth not shine, there is neither prosperity nor health, *The doctrine to be taken of this psalm.*

neither strength nor comfort, either in body or soul; but utter disquietness, terror, and despair, specially when trouble, distress, and painful death is at hand. Howbeit the un-
Isai. lvii. godly, as the prophet saith, have never rest, whether they be in wealth or woe. For if they be in prosperity, then are they presumptuous, proud, and high-minded, forget our Lord God utterly, boast and crack only of their own power, riches, wisdom, &c.; and take thought beside, how they may maintain and increase the same, and how they may persecute and oppress other men that lie in their ways. But if the leaf turn about with them, as doubtless it must
Deposuit potentes de sede, et divites dimisit inanes. needs do at the last; (for that sweet virgin Mary is a very sure prophetess, which yet hath not failed in her song;) then are they of all the most miserable and carefullest people, which immediately fall to despair and mistrust. What aileth them? They know not where nor how they shall seek comfort, seeing they have not the word of God, which alone teacheth the right way how to be patient, and to have a good hope even in adversity. Rom. xv.

An ensample for us. This thing ought to warn us and move us, that we esteem nothing more excellent nor worthy upon earth, than this benefit, namely, to have that dear blessed word, and that we can be in a place where it may be freely preached and professed openly. A christian man therefore, that belongeth unto a church wherein the word of God is taught, as oft as he goeth in, should think upon this psalm, and out of a joyful heart with the prophet to give God thanks for his unoutspeakable grace, that he hath set him, as his own sheep, in a pleasant green meadow, where there is plenty of good grass and fresh water; that is, that he may be in a place where he may hear and learn the word of God, and conceive rich comfort thereout, both in body and soul.

This blessed David did well understand, how worthy a treasure it is, when it may be so had: therefore can he boast and sing so well of it, and magnify this benefit above all that
What we ought to learn here of David. is in any estimation or worship upon earth. At him ought we to learn this science, and according to his ensample not only to be thankful unto God our loving and faithful shepherd, and to magnify his unoutspeakable gift, which he of very loving-kindness hath given us, as David doth here in the first five verses; but also earnestly to desire and pray

him, as he doth in the last verse, that he may abide by his riches, and never to fall away from his holy christian church.

And such a prayer is exceeding necessary: for we are very weak, and, as the apostle St Paul saith, we carry this treasure about in earthen vessels. The devil also, our adversary, beareth deadly hate unto us for this treasure's sake. Therefore doth he not rest, but goeth about as a roaring lion, and seeketh how he may devour us. Beside all this, he hath a quarrel unto us, because of our old sack which we carry yet upon our necks, wherein there be yet also divers concupiscences and sins. Moreover, the dear flock of Christ is spotted and filled with so many horrible offences, or slanders, that because of the same there do many fall away from them. Therefore, I say, it is necessary that we pray, and put this uncorrupt doctrine still in practice, and defend ourselves therewith against all slanders, that we may continue unto the end, and be saved.

2 Cor. v.

This mad and blind world knoweth utterly nothing of this treasure and precious stone, but imagineth only, even as a swine or unreasonable beast, how they may here fill the belly; or else, when it cometh to the point, they follow lies and hypocrisy: as for the truth and faith, they let it pass. Therefore do they sing no psalm unto God for his holy word; but rather, when he offereth it unto them, they blaspheme it and condemn it for heresy. And as for those that teach it or will be known of it, the world persecuteth them and putteth them to death, like as if they were deceivers, and the most ungracious wretches that are in the world. It shall be good therefore for this small flock to acknowledge such a benefit, and with the prophet to sing a psalm or song of thanksgiving unto God for it.

The blindness of the world.

But what say ye of them that cannot have the preaching of God's word; as namely, they that dwell here and there among tyrants and enemies of the truth? No doubt, where as the word of God is preached, there can it not pass away without fruit, as Esay saith in the fifty-fifth chapter. The good christian people also of the same place have one vantage, which indeed is dear unto them: for they that be christian men count it a very great thing, that they may be in a place where the word of God is freely and openly taught

Of them that would and cannot have the word of God.

and knowledged, and the sacraments ministered after Christ's institution. But as for those, they be sown very thin. The false Christian are always more than the good. The great multitude careth nothing for God's word, neither do they knowledge it for a benefit, that they may hear it without all harm and peril. Yea, they are soon filled and weary of it, and esteem it but a pain to hear it, and to receive the holy sacrament.

Again, they that suffer under tyrants complain day and night, and long greatly for it. And if a small morsel of our bread, that Christ hath given us so richly, doth come unto them, they receive it with great joy and thankfulness, and do themselves much good withal; whereas our swine in the mean season, having that worthy bread themselves so richly, and many whole baskets full thereof, cannot reach unto it, they are so weary of it. Yea, they cast it down, wallow themselves therein, tread it under their feet, and run over it.

Men wear weary of the word of God. Therefore goeth it even after the proverb. When a thing beginneth to be common, it is no more set by, but despised, be it never so precious. And such proverbs are specially found true in the word of God. Where men have it, there will they not away withal. Again, where men have it not, there would they be glad to have it. Where men have a church at their doors wherein the word of God is taught, there go they up and down in the market in the preaching time, and lurk about the graves. Where they be ten or twenty miles from it, there would they be glad to go with the multitude, and to pass over with them unto the house of God with joyfulness and thanksgiving, [Psalm xlii.] as it is in the forty-first psalm.

Of them that dwell under tyrants. Therefore shortly this is mine answer unto the question concerning them that dwell under tyrants. Blessed be they which are now scattered abroad under the Turk or pope, being destitute of God's word, and would yet be glad with all their hearts to have it, and in the mean season receive with thanksgiving such morsels as they can get, till the meal be better. Now if they be not far from the place where the word of God is preached, and the blessed sacrament ministered according unto Christ's institution, they may well go thither and enjoy the same treasure, like as many do, and are therefore punished of their wicked rulers, both in body and goods. But if they dwell far from such places, yet do they not cease at the least to sigh thereafter. No doubt Christ our Lord will hear their sighing, and in process of time will he turn back their captivity. Again, unhappy, yea, and unhappy again are they that have this treasure plenteously at their doors, and yet care not for it. On them shall the word of Christ be fulfilled, where he saith: "Many shall come from the east and west, and shall sit with Abraham, Isaac, and Jacob in the kingdom of heaven; but the children of the kingdom shall be cast out," &c. _{Matt. viii.}

Let this be said for an introduction. Now will we shortly go over the psalm.

The Lord is my shepherd: I shall lack nothing.

First of all, the prophet and every faithful heart calleth God his shepherd. Now though the scripture giveth God many loving names, yet this which the prophet giveth here unto God is a much more sweet and gracious name, where he calleth him a shepherd, and saith: "The Lord is my shepherd." _{A sweet name.}

It is very comfortable, when the scripture calleth God our hope, our strength, our stony rock, our castle, our shield, our comfort, our deliverer, our king, &c.; for verily he declareth the thing so still indeed unto his own, that he is even so as the scripture describeth him. But exceeding comfortable is it, that he is called here, and many times else in the scripture, a "shepherd." For in this word alone, "shepherd," is almost all comprehended together, what good and comforting thing soever is spoken of God.

Therefore doth the prophet speak this word with a joyful and sorrowless heart, which is full of faith, and for very great gladness and comfort exceedeth; and saith not, "The Lord is my strength, castle," &c., which were a marvellous comforting saying; but, "the Lord is my shepherd." As if he would say: If the Lord be my shepherd and I his sheep, then am I wondrous well provided for, both in body and soul: he shall get me a competent living; he shall defend me and keep me from misfortune; he shall care for me; he shall help me out of all trouble; he shall comfort me; he shall strengthen me, &c. Summa, he shall do for me whatsoever a good shepherd ought to do. All these benefits _{The cause that moved the prophet to call God his shepherd.}

and more doth he comprehend in this only word "shepherd," as he expoundeth it himself immediately, where he saith: "I shall lack nothing."

Besides this, some of the other names which the scripture ascribes unto God, sound partly too glorious and too high, and bring in a manner of fear with them, when men hear them to be named; as when the scripture calleth God our Lord, King, Maker, &c.

Of such a nature is not this word "shepherd," but soundeth very friendly; and unto them that be godly it bringeth in a manner a confidence, comfort, and trust with it, when they read or hear it; like as this word "Father," and other more, when they be appropriated unto God.

<small>A very comfortable similitude.</small> Therefore is this one of the most loving and comforting similitudes, and yet very common in the scripture, that it likeneth the majesty of God to a virtuous, faithful, or, as Christ saith, a good shepherd; and us poor, weak, and wretched sinners to a sheep.

Now cannot this comforting and loving similitude be better understand, than to go into the creatures themselves, whereout the prophets take this and such other like similitudes; and to learn diligently thereby, what the condition and property of a natural sheep is, and the office, labour, and diligence of a good shepherd. Whoso taketh good heed thereunto, may not only with ease understand this and other similitudes in the scripture concerning the shepherd and the sheep; but also they shall be unto him exceeding sweet and comforting.

<small>The condition of a sheep.</small> A sheep must live only by the help, defence, and diligence of his shepherd. As soon as it leaveth him, it is compassed about with all manner of peril, and must needs perish; for it cannot help itself. For why? it is a poor, weak, and innocent beast, that can neither feed nor guide itself, nor find the right way, nor keep itself against any unhappiness or misfortune; seeing this, that of nature it is fearful, flieth and goeth astray. And if it go but a little out of the way, and come from his shepherd, it is not possible for itself to find him again, but runneth ever farther and farther from him. And though it come to other shepherds and sheep, yet is it nothing helped therewith: for it knoweth not the voice of strange shepherds; therefore flieth it from them,

and runneth so long astray, till the wolf ravish it, or till it perish some other ways.

Nevertheless, as weak a beast as it is, yet has it this condition, that with all diligence it bideth with his own shepherd, and seeketh comfort at his help and defence; and how or whither soever he leadeth it, it followeth. And if it can but be with him, it careth for no more, neither feareth it any man, but is careless and merry; for it lacketh nothing. It hath also this good virtue in it, which is well to be marked, (for Christ doth specially praise the same in his sheep;) this virtue, I say, it hath, that it will be earnest and sure to hear and know the voice of his shepherd, and ordereth itself thereafter, and will for nothing go from it, but followeth straight the same. Again, it regardeth no strange shepherd's voice: and though they call and whistle upon it never so friendly, yet careth not it therefore; much less doth it follow them.

The property of a sheep.

Again, this is the office of a good shepherd, that he doth not only provide for his sheep pasture, and other more things that belong thereto, but defendeth them also, that no harm chance unto them. Besides this, he taketh diligent heed that he lese none. If any go astray, he runneth after it, seeketh it, and fetcheth it again. As for such as be young, feeble, and sick, he dealeth gently with them, keepeth them, holdeth them up, and carrieth them, till they be old, strong, and whole, &c.

The office of a shepherd.

Even thus goeth it also in the spiritual sheepfold, that is to say, in the flock of Christ. Look, how little a natural sheep can keep, guide, rule, save, or defend itself against danger and misfortune, (for it is a feeble and weaponless beast;) so little can we poor, weak, and miserable people keep and rule ourselves spiritually, walk and endure in the right way, or of our own strength to defend us against all evil, and to get us help and comfort in trouble and distress.

How it goeth in the sheep-fold of Christ.

For how should he have skill to guide himself after a godly fashion, that knoweth nothing of God, that is conceived and born in sin (as we all are), and of nature the child of wrath and the enemy of God? How should we find the right way, and continue therein, seeing that (as the prophet Esay saith) we can do nothing but go astray? How is it possible that we should defend ourselves from the devil,

The misery of our nature.

which is a prince and lord of this world, whose prisoners also we be every one, seeing that with all power and might we cannot do so much as to hinder a small leaf to hurt us, or a poor flea from grieving us? Why will we poor wretched people boast so much of great comfort, help, and counsel against the judgment of God, against God's wrath and everlasting death, seeing that by ourselves and others we have experience daily and hourly, how we can neither counsel nor comfort ourselves in small bodily necessities?

A plain comparison. Therefore conclude thus hardly: as little as a natural sheep can help itself in the things that be least of all, but must look for all benefits at his shepherd's hand; much less can a man rule, comfort, help, or give counsel unto himself in things belonging to salvation, but must look for all such only at the hand of God his shepherd; which to fulfil anything for his sheep that is to be done is a thousand times more willing and diligent, than any other virtuous shepherd in the world.

Christ is our shepherd. As for this shepherd, of whom the prophet had spoken so long before, it is even Christ our loving master, which is far another manner of shepherd than Moses, which is hard and extreme unto his sheep, and driveth them back into the wilderness, where they find neither pasture nor water, but plain scarceness, Exod. iii. But Christ is the gracious and loving shepherd, which runneth after the famished and lost sheep in the wilderness, and seeketh it there; "and when he findeth it, he taketh it up gladly upon his shoulders," Luke xv.; yea, "and giveth his life also for his sheep," John x. This must needs be a loving shepherd. Who would not be glad then to be a sheep of his?

The shepherd's voice. This shepherd's voice, wherewith he speaketh and calleth unto his sheep, is the holy gospel, whereby we be taught that we obtain grace, remission of sins, and everlasting salvation, not by Moses' law, (wherethrough he putteth us in the more fear, dread, and despair, which were too fearful, too sore afraid, and despaired too much afore,) but by Christ, which is "the shepherd and bishop of our souls," 1 Pet. ii.; which hath sought us miserable and lost sheep, and fetched us out of the wilderness, that is to say, from the law, from sin, from death, from the power of the devil, from everlasting damnation; and in that he gave his life for us, obtained he us grace, remission of sins, comfort, help, and strength against the devil and all misfortune, yea, and everlasting life also. This is now unto the sheep of Christ a loving sweet voice, which they are heartily glad to hear, which they know right well, and order themselves thereafter. "As for a strange voice that soundeth otherwise, they neither know it nor hearken unto it, but avoid and flee away from it," &c. John x.

The pasture, wherewith Christ feedeth his sheep, is also the comforting gospel, whereby the souls are fed and strengthened, kept from error, comforted in all temptations and troubles, defended against the craft and power of the devil, and finally delivered out of all trouble. Nevertheless, forasmuch as his sheep are not all alike strong, but some yet lost and scattered here and there abroad, wounded, sick, young, and feeble; he doth not therefore cast them away, but hath much more respect unto them, and careth more diligently for them, than for the other that have no such need. For as the prophet Ezekiel saith in the xxxivth chapter: "He seeketh them that be lost, bringeth together them that be scattered abroad, bindeth up such as be wounded, looketh to them that be sick." And the weak lambs that be but young at the first, saith Esay, "he taketh up in his arms, and beareth them, and such as be with young ones doth he drive forth fair and softly." All this doth our loving master Christ by the office of preaching and distributing of the holy sacrament; as it is oft and with many words taught in other places. For to set it forth here word by word as need should require, it were too long. The prophet also himself will declare it afterward in the psalm.

<small>The pasture.</small>

By this then may we easily perceive, how shamefully we have been seduced under the papacy. For Christ was not so lovingly set forth unto us as the dearly beloved prophets, apostles, and Christ himself doth: but so fearfully was he described unto us, that we have been more afraid of him than of Moses; yea, we thought Moses' doctrine much more lighter, and to have much more sweetness in it, than the doctrine of Christ. And so we knew nothing else, but that Christ had been a wrathful judge, whose displeasure we might have reconciled with our good works and with our

<small>We have been deceived.</small>

holiness, and whose pardon we might have obtained through the merits and intercessions of saints. This is not only a shameful lesson, and a miserable deceiving of poor consciences, but also the highest blasphemy of the grace of God, a denying of the death, resurrection, and ascension of Christ, &c., and of all his unoutspeakable benefits, slandering and condemning of his holy gospel, a destroying of faith, and instead thereof a setting up of utter abominations, lies, and errors, &c.

Blindness. If this be not darkness, then cannot I tell what darkness is. Yet could no man in a manner perceive it, but every man took it for the plain verity; and yet unto this day will our papists needs take it for the right way, and shed much innocent blood for the same. Go to then, if we can preserve ourselves from error, if we can obtain grace and remission of sins, resist the devil and all misfortune, overcome sin and death by our own merits; then must all the scripture be false, which testifieth of us, how that of ourselves we are but lost, scattered abroad, wounded, weak, and feeble sheep. And so should we have no need of Christ to be shepherd, to seek us, to bring us together, to guide us, to bind us up, to look upon us, and to strengthen us against the devil. And so hath he also given his life for us in vain. For if we can bring all this to pass, and obtain it through our own strength and goodness, then have we no need of Christ's help.

Mark this well. But here thou hearest the contrary, namely, that thou art but a lost sheep, and of thyself canst not come to the shepherd again; but to go astray, only that canst thou well do. And if Christ thy shepherd did not seek and fetch thee again, thou must needs be a prey unto the wolf. But now he cometh, seeketh, findeth, and bringeth thee unto his fold, that is to say, into his christian congregation, through the word and sacrament; giveth his life for thee, and holdeth thee still by the right hand, lest thou shouldest fall into any error. There hearest thou nothing of thine own strength, of thine own good works and merits; except thou wilt call it strength, a good work, and merit, to go astray, to be feeble and lost. Christ worketh, deserveth, and sheweth here his power only. It is he that seeketh, beareth, and guideth thee. He through his death deserveth life for thee. He only is strong, and defendeth thee, lest thou shouldest perish and be taken away out of his hands. John x. Unto all this canst thou do nothing, save apply thine ears to hear, and with thanksgiving to receive such an unoutspeakable treasure, and to learn to know well the voice of the shepherd, to follow him, and to eschew the voice of strangers. Wherefore, if thou wilt be richly provided for, both in body and soul, above all things take good heed then to the voice of this shepherd; hearken well what he saith unto thee; let him feed thee, rule thee, guide thee, defend thee, comfort thee, &c.: that is to say, keep thee unto his word, be glad to hear it and to learn it, and so no doubt thou shalt be well provided for, both in body and soul. *Take heed to thy shepherd's voice.*

By this that hath been spoken of hitherto, I think it but easy to understand these words, "The Lord is my shepherd;" yea, and all the whole psalm beside. They are but few words: "THE LORD IS MY SHEPHERD;" but a great weight and pith. The world maketh great boasting and cracking of honour, power, riches, favour of men, &c. But the prophet maketh his boast of none of these; for they be all uncertain and transitory. He speaketh but few words and good: "The Lord is my shepherd." Thus speaketh a sure and constant faith; which turneth her back upon everything that is temporal and transitory, how high and precious soever it be; and turneth the face and heart straight unto the Lord, which is only and altogether, and doth it himself alone. Even he, and else none, whether he be king or emperor, saith he, "is my shepherd." Therefore goeth he forward in all quietness, and saith:

I shall lack nothing.

This doth he speak in general of all the benefits bodily and ghostly, that we receive by the office of preaching. As though he would say: That the Lord be my shepherd, then doubtless I shall lack nothing; I shall have abundance of meat, drink, clothing, a living, defence, peace, and all manner of necessaries, whatsoever serveth for the sustentation of this life: for I have a rich shepherd, which shall not suffer me to lack. Nevertheless he doth speak most specially of the spiritual goods and gifts, that the word of God bringeth with it, and saith: 'Forasmuch as the Lord hath taken me among his flock, and provideth for me with his own pasture, *A general sentence.*

that is, forasmuch as he hath richly given me his holy word, he shall not suffer me to have scarceness in any thing. He shall give his blessing unto the word, that it may have strength, and bring forth fruit in me. He shall likewise give me his Spirit, to stand by me and to comfort me in all temptations and troubles, to make my heart also sure and certain, and that I doubt not therein, but that I am one of my shepherd's dear sheep, and he my faithful shepherd, which will deal gently with me, as with a poor weak sheep, and will strengthen my faith, endue me also with other spiritual gifts, comfort me in all troubles, hear me when I call upon him, defend me from the wolf, that is, from the devil, so that he shall not be able to do me harm; and finally deliver me from all misfortune.'

I shall lack nothing.

An objection. Thou wilt say, Yea, and whereby shall I perceive that the Lord is my shepherd? I cannot perceive that he dealeth so lovingly with me, as the psalm speaketh; yea, the contrary do I well perceive. David was an holy prophet, and a man dearly beloved unto God: therefore could he easily talk of the matter, and believe well as he said. As for me, I shall not be able to do it after him; for I am a poor sinner.

An answer. I have declared above, that a sheep hath this good condition and proper virtue in it, that it knoweth well the voice of his shepherd, and ordereth itself rather after the ears, than after the eyes. The same virtue doth Christ praise also in his sheep, when he saith, (John x.) "My sheep know my voice." Now his voice soundeth after this manner: "I am a good shepherd, and give my life for my sheep. And I give them everlasting life, and they shall never perish, and no man shall pluck them out of my hand." Take good heed now unto this voice, and order thyself thereafter: if thou do so, then be sure that thou art one of Christ's sheep, and he thy shepherd, which knoweth thee right well, and can call thee by name. Now if thou hast him for thy shepherd, then shalt thou verily lack nothing; yea, thou hast already that thou shouldest have, even everlasting life. Item, thou shalt never perish, neither shall there be any power so great and mighty, as to be able to pluck thee out of his hand. Only be thou sure of this: for doubtless this shepherd's voice shall never fail thee. What wilt thou more? But if thou lettest this voice go, and orderest thyself after the sight of the eyes and after the feeling of that old Adam; then leseth thou the faith and confidence, which thou as a sheep shouldest have unto him, as to thy shepherd. And so falleth thee upon the now one imagination, now another, so that thou canst not be in quiet, but disputest by thyself, and sayest: If the Lord be my shepherd, why suffereth he then the world to plague me and persecute me too miserably, contrary to all my deserving? I sit among wolves, and am not sure of my life the twinkling of an eye; but I see no shepherd that will defend me. Item, why giveth he the devil licence to do me so much harm with fear and despair? Besides this, I find myself all unapt, feeble, unpatient, and laden yet with many sins; I find no certainty, but doubtfulness; no consolation, but fearfulness and quaking for the wrath of God. When beginneth he to declare to me, that he is my shepherd?

Leave not the voice of thy shepherd.

Such and many other no wonderful cogitations shalt thou have, if thou let his voice and word pass. But if thou cleave still fast unto it, then sufferest thou neither the deceitfulness of the devil, the displeasure and madness of the world, neither thine own infirmity and unworthiness, to overcome thee by temptation; but goest on boldly, and sayest, Whether the devil, the world, or mine own conscience do take part against me never so fiercely, yet will not I therefore take overmuch thought. It must and shall be thus, that whosoever is a sheep of the Lord, he cannot remain untempted. Let it go with me as it may, yea, whether they seethe me or roast me, yet is this my comfort, that my shepherd hath given his life for me. Besides this, he hath also a sweet and loving voice, wherewith he comforteth, and saith, I shall never perish, neither shall there any man pluck me out of his hand, but I shall have everlasting life. This promise will be faithfully kept with me, whatsoever become of me. And though sometime there chance a sin or other impediment by the reason of mine infirmity, yet will he not therefore cast me away; for he is a loving shepherd, which looketh to the weak sheep, bindeth up their wounds, and healeth them. And to the

What good followeth when one cleaveth fast to God's words.

intent that I should be the surer of this, and not to doubt thereon, he hath left me here the holy sacrament, for a token that it is so indeed.

Even thus hath the prophet done. He was not merry always, neither could he at all hours sing, "The Lord is my shepherd, I shall lack nothing." He hath been sometime at many a great exigent, yea, all too many; so that he neither felt the righteousness, comfort, nor help of God, but plain sin, the wrath of God, fearfulness, despair, the pains of hell, &c.; as he complaineth himself in many psalms. Nevertheless he turneth him from his own feeling, and taketh hold of God by his promise concerning Messias that then was for to come, and casteth this in his mind: 'Howsoever it stand with me, yet is this the comfort of my heart, that I have a gracious and merciful Lord, which is my shepherd, whose word and promise doth strengthen and comfort me; therefore shall I lack nothing.' And even therefore hath he written this and other psalms, to the intent that we should be sure, that in very temptations there is elsewhere no counsel and comfort to be found; and that this is the only golden science, namely, to cleave unto the word and promise of God, and to judge after the same, and not after the feeling of the heart. And so, no doubt, there shall follow help and comfort, and not fail in anything.

Now followeth the second verse.

He feedeth me in a green pasture, and leadeth me to the fresh water.

In the first verse hath the prophet shortly comprehended the meaning of the whole psalm, namely, that whosoever hath the Lord for his shepherd shall lack nothing. More than this doth not he teach in this psalm; but only setteth forth the same more at large with goodly ornate words and similitudes, how it chanceth that they which are the Lord's sheep lack nothing, and saith: "He feedeth me," &c. But almost throughout the whole psalm (as his manner is ofttimes to do) he useth words, which signify somewhat else than they sound. As when he maketh mention of the shepherd, of the feeding of the green pasture, of the fresh water, the staff, the sheep-hook, &c., it is easy to perceive, that he will have somewhat else understood thereby than we men use to speak thereof. Such manner of speaking is very common in the scripture; and therefore should man take diligent heed thereunto, that they may be accustomed withal, and learn to understand it.

But see how well-favouredly he can speak. I am, saith he, a sheep of the Lord's, which feedeth me in a green pasture, &c. A natural sheep cannot be better than when the shepherd feedeth it in a pleasant green pasture, and beside fresh water. If it can have this, it thinketh no man upon earth is more rich or happier than it; for there it findeth every thing that it can desire: a goodly thick plentiful grass, whereof it waxeth strong and fat; a fresh water, wherewith it can refresh and quicken itself. There hath it pleasure and joy. Even so will David say here likewise, that God never shewed him a greater grace and benefit upon earth than this, that he might be in the place and among the people, where the word and dwelling of God and the right God's service was. For where that treasure is, there goeth it well both in the spiritual and worldly regiment. As if he would say: 'All the nations and kingdoms upon earth are nothing. They are indeed richer, mightier, and more glorious than we Jews, and make great boasting thereof. They boast also of their wisdom and holiness, for they have gods also whom they serve: yet with all their pomp and glory, they are but even a plain wilderness and desert. For there is neither shepherd nor pasture; therefore must the sheep needs stray, be famished, and perish. As for us, though we have many wildernesses about us, yet sit we here at rest, safe and merry in paradise, and in a pleasant green pasture, where there is plenty of grass and fresh water, and have with us our shepherd, which feedeth us, leadeth us to the drink, defendeth us, &c. Therefore can we lack nothing.'

This man had spiritual eyes, and therefore saw he right well what is the best and noblest good upon earth. He maketh no boast of his kingly worship and power: he knowledgeth well, that such goods are also the gifts of God; neither runneth he from them, and letteth them lie, but useth them unto the honour of God, and giveth him thanks therefore. But of this maketh he specially his boast, namely, that the Lord is his shepherd, and he in his pasture and feeding; that is, that he hath God's word. This benefit

_{The chiefest good upon earth is to have God's word.}

can he never forget; but speaketh thereof marvellous excellently, and with great joy, and praiseth it far above all the goods upon earth. And this he doth in many psalms, as in the 118th, where he saith: "The law of thy mouth is dearer unto me than thousands of gold and silver." Item: "I love thy commandments above gold and precious stone. O how sweet are thy words unto my throat! Yea, more than honey unto my mouth."

[Psal. cxix.]

<small>What we ought here to learn.</small>

This science should we learn also, namely, to let the world boast of their great riches, honour, power, &c. For it is loose, uncertain, and transitory ware, which God casteth into the dungeon. It is a small matter for him to give an ungracious person, that blasphemeth and dishonoureth him again, for his reward, a kingdom, a dukedom, or any other worship and good upon earth. These worldly goods are his draff and swillings, wherewith he filleth the hogs' bellies, that he is disposed to kill. But unto his children, as David speaketh here thereof, he giveth the right treasure. Therefore should we, as the dear children and heirs of God, neither boast ourselves of our wisdom, strength, nor riches, but of this, that we have the precious pearl, even that worthy word, whereby we know God our loving Father, and Jesus Christ whom he hath sent. This is our treasure and inheritance, which is sure and everlasting, and better than all the good of the world. Whoso hath this, let him suffer other men to gather money together, to live voluptuously, to be proud and high-minded: but though he himself be despised and poor in the sight of the world, yet let not that tempt him; but let him thank God for his unoutspeakable gift, and pray that he may abide thereby. It maketh no matter how rich and glorious we be here upon earth; if we keep this treasure, we have plenty of riches and honour. St Paul was a man of light reputation, and poor upon earth, having the devil and the world very fierce against him: but in the sight of God he was a man right dear, and greatly set by. Besides this, he was so poor, that he was fain to get his living with the labour of his hands. And yet for all that great poverty he was richer than the emperor of Rome; having nevertheless none other riches but the knowledge of Christ. "For the which," saith he, Phil. iii. "I count all things nothing upon earth, except very loss and dung."

<small>The word of God is our treasure.</small>

The God of mercy grant us grace, that we also, after the ensample of David, Paul, and other holy men, may count our treasure, which is even the same that they had, as great, and magnify it above all the goods upon earth, and heartily to give God thanks therefore, that he hath vouchsafed it upon us afore many thousands of other! He might have suffered us to go astray, as well as the Turks, Egyptians, Jews, and other idolaters, which know not of that treasure; or else he might have suffered us still to be hard-hearted, as are the papists, that blaspheme and condemn this treasure of ours: whereas he hath set us now in his own green meadow, and provided us so richly with good pasture and fresh water. It cometh even of his grace; therefore have we the more to thank him for. *God hath done more for us than for many other.*

As for the people of God, or the holy congregation of Christ, the prophet calleth it a green meadow. For it is a pleasant garden, garnished and beautified with all manner of spiritual gifts. The pasture or grass therein is the word of God, whereby the consciences are strengthened and refreshed. In the same green meadow doth our Lord God gather his sheep together, feedeth them therein with good grass, and refresheth them with fresh water: that is, he committeth unto the holy christian church the shepherd's office, delivereth and giveth her the holy gospel and the sacraments, to take charge and look to his sheep therewith, that they may be richly provided for with doctrine, with comfort, with strength, and with defence against all evil, &c. As for those that preach the law of Moses, or the commandments of men, they feed not the sheep in a green pasture, but in the wilderness, where they famish, and lead them to foul stinking waters, whereof they perish and die. *The meadow. The grass. What they be that feed sheep in the wilderness.*

By this allegory of the green pasture will the prophet declare the great abundance and riches of the holy gospel and of the knowledge of Christ among the faithful. For like as the grass in a green meadow standeth goodly thick and full, and ever groweth more and more; even so have the faithful not only God's word with all plenteousness, but also the more they use and meddle withal, the more it increaseth and groweth among them. Therefore setteth he the words marvellous plainly. *The great riches of such as believe.*

He saith not, he bringeth me once or oft into a green

pasture; but feedeth me still therein, that I may lie, take my rest, and dwell even in the midst of the grass, and need never to suffer hunger or any scarceness beside. For the word that he here useth may be called lying, or resting, as a beast lieth and resteth upon his four feet. After the same manner [Psal. lxxii.] doth Solomon speak also in the seventy-first psalm, where he prophesieth of the kingdom of Christ and the gospel, that it should mightily go through and come into all places, and saith: "There shall be an heap of corn in the earth high upon the hills, &c., and shall be green in the city, like grass upon the earth." That David also in this psalm speaketh likewise of the gospel, he declareth himself afterward, when he saith: "He quickeneth my soul." Item: "Thy staff and thy sheep-hook do comfort me."

<small>The first fruit of God's word.</small> This is now the first fruit of the word of God, that the christians are so instructed thereby, that they increase in faith and hope, learn to commit all their doings unto God, and whatsoever they have need of, either in soul or body, to look for it at his hand, &c.

And leadeth me to the fresh water.

<small>The second fruit of God's word.</small> This is the second fruit of God's word. It is unto the faithful not only pasture and grass, whereby they are filled and strengthened in faith; but it is also unto them a goodly cold fresh water, whereby they take refreshing and comfort. Therefore leaveth he not there where he said, "He feedeth me in a green pasture;" but addeth this also unto it, "And leadeth me to the fresh water." As if he would say: In the [Psal. cxxi.] great heat, when the sun doth sore burn (Psal. cxx.), and I can have no shadow, then leadeth he me to the fresh water, giveth me drink and refresheth me: that is, in all manner of troubles, anguishes, and necessities, ghostly and bodily, when I know not elsewhere to find help or comfort, I hold me unto the word of grace. There only, and nowhere else, do I find the right consolation and refreshing, and that plenteously. Now, whereas he speaketh here of this comfort with garnished words, he talketh of it in another place with plain and mani-
<small>Psal. cxviii. [cxix.]</small> fest words, and saith: "If thy word were not my comfort and delight, I should perish in my trouble." "I will never forget thy word, for in my trouble it is my consolation; yea, thy word quickeneth me."

Nevertheless he continueth still in the similitude of the shepherd and of the sheep; and, no doubt, it is common in all the prophets. For of the sheep and other cattle had the Jews their best living, and were commonly shepherds, as was David and the patriarchs. Therefore is this similitude ofttimes spoken of in the scripture. But David speaketh of this matter after the nature of the country. For the land of promise is an hot, dry, sandy, and stony land, which hath many wildernesses and little water. Therefore in the first book of Moses it was more than once declared, how that the heathen shepherds strove with the shepherds of the patriarchs because of water. For the which cause in the same country they take it for a special treasure, if they might have water for their cattle. In our countries we know not thereof; for there is water enough every where. Of this did David see, and he rehearseth it for a special benefit, to be under the custody of the Lord, which should not only feed him in a green pasture, but also in the heat bringing him to the fresh water, &c. *Why the scripture rehearseth so oft this similitude.*

Shortly, his meaning is to declare, that as little as a man can come to the knowledge of God and the truth, and to the right faith, without the word of God; so little can there be any comfort and peace of conscience be found without the same. The worldly have also their comfort and joy; howbeit that endureth but the twinkling of an eye: when trouble and anguish cometh, and specially the last hour, it goeth away; as Solomon saith: "After laughter cometh sorrow, and after joy cometh heaviness." But as for them that drink of this fresh and living water, they may well suffer trouble and disease in the world; but they shall never lack the true consolation. And specially when it cometh to the point, the leaf turneth over with them: which is as much to say as, 'After short weeping cometh everlasting laughter, and after a little sorrow cometh excellent joy.' 2 Cor. v. For they shall not weep and mourn both here and there; but, as Christ saith: "Blessed are you that weep here, for ye shall laugh." Luke vi. *Without God's word can no man's conscience be at rest.* Prov. xiv.

He quickeneth my soul, and bringeth me forth in the way of righteousness for his name's sake.

Here doth the prophet declare himself, of what manner of pasture and fresh water he spake, namely, even of the *Spiritual pasture and water.*

same that strengtheneth and quickeneth the soul. This can be nothing else but God's word. But forasmuch as our Lord God hath two manner of words, the law and the gospel, the prophet, when he saith, "He quickeneth my soul," giveth sufficiently to understand, that he speaketh not here of the law, but of the gospel. The law cannot quicken the soul; for it is a word that requireth and commandeth us to love God with all our hearts, &c., and our neighbour as ourselves. Whoso doth not this, him it condemneth, and speaketh this sentence over him: "Cursed be every man which doth not all that is written in the book of the law." Deut. xxvii. Gal. iii. Now is it certain, that no man upon earth doth this; therefore cometh the law with his judgment, fearing and vexing the consciences: and if there be no help, it goeth through; so that they must needs fall into despair, and be condemned for ever. Of this occasion doth St Paul say: "By the law cometh but the knowledge of sin." Item, "The law causeth but wrath."

<small>The law.</small>

<small>Rom. iii.</small>
<small>Rom. iv.</small>
<small>The gospel.</small>

As for the gospel, it is a blessed word; it requireth none such of us, but bringeth us tidings of all good, namely, that God hath given us poor sinners his only Son, to be our shepherd, to seek again us famished and dispersed sheep, and to give his life for us, that he might so deliver us from sin, from everlasting death, and from the power of the devil. This is the green grass, and the fresh water, wherewith the Lord quickeneth our souls. And thus are we made loose from evil consciences and heavy thoughts. Of this shall we speak more in the fourth verse.

He bringeth me forth in the way of righteousness.

Here, saith he, doth not the Lord my faithful shepherd leave, that he feedeth me in a green meadow, and leadeth me to the fresh water, and so quickeneth my soul; but he bringeth me forth also in the right way, that I depart not aside, go astray, and so perish: that is, he holdeth me fast to the pure doctrine, that I be not deceived by false spirits, and that I fall not away by any other temptation or offence; item, that I may know how I ought to lead mine outward conversation and life, and that I suffer not myself to be persuaded by the holiness and strait life of hypocrites; item, what is the true doctrine, faith, and service of God, &c.

<small>To be led in the right way what it is.</small>

This is now again a goodly fruit and virtue of the word of God, that they which cleave fast thereunto, do not only receive strength and comfort of soul thereby, but are preserved also from untrue doctrine and false holiness. Many men obtain this treasure, but they cannot keep it. For as soon as a man is too bold and presumptuous, and thinketh himself sure of the matter, it is done with him: or ever he can look about him, he is deceived. For the devil also can pretend holiness, and transform himself into an angel of light, as St Paul saith: and even so likewise can his ministers shew themselves, as though they were the preachers of righteousness, and come in sheep's clothing among the flock of Christ, but inwardly are they ravening wolves. Therefore is it good here to watch and pray, as the prophet doth in the last verse, that our shepherd may keep us by this treasure which he hath given us. They that do not this, certainly they shall lose it. "And the end of that man," as Christ saith, "shall be worse than the beginning." For they shall afterward become the most poisoned enemies of Christ's flock, and do more harm with their false doctrine than the tyrants with the sword. This had St Paul well proved by the false apostles, that made the Corinthians and Galatians to err so soon, and afterward made division in all Asia. We see it ourselves also this day by the anabaptists and other false spirits.

An excellent virtue of God's word.

Luke xi.

For his name's sake.

The name of God is the preaching of God, whereby he is magnified and known to be gracious, merciful, long-suffering, true, faithful, &c.; which, notwithstanding that we be the children of wrath, and guilty of everlasting death, forgiveth us all our sins, and taketh us for his own children and inheritors. This is his name, this doth he cause to be proclaimed by his word. Thus will he be known, magnified, and honoured; and, according unto the first commandment, he will even thus declare himself toward us, as he hath caused it to be preached of him: like as he doth still, strengtheneth and quickeneth our souls spiritually, and keepeth us that we fall not into error, getteth us living for our body, and preserveth us from all misfortune.

The name of God.

This honour, that he so is as we have now said, is given

him only by them that cleave fast unto his word: these believe and confess plainly, that all the gifts and goods which they have, spiritual and bodily, they receive them of God, even of his mere grace and goodness; that is to say, "For his name's sake," not for their own work and deservings. For this do they give thanks unto him, and declare the same unto others. This honour cannot be given unto God by any presumptuous justiciaries, as heretics and false spirits, or enemies and blasphemers of God's word; for they magnify not his name, but their own.

And though I walk in the valley of the shadow of death, yet fear I no evil; for thou art with me: thy staff, thy sheep-hook do comfort me.

Hitherto hath the prophet declared, that they which have and love the word of God can lack nothing. For the Lord is their shepherd, which doth not only feed them in a green pasture and leadeth them to the fresh water, that they may be fat, strong, and refreshed both bodily and spiritually; but also taketh such care for them, that they be not weary of the good pasture and fresh water, leaving the green meadow, and depart again from the right way into the wilderness. This is the first part of this psalm. Now teacheth he farther, how that they which are the sheep of this shepherd be compassed about with many jeopardies and misfortunes. Nevertheless the Lord, saith he, not only defendeth them, but delivereth them also out of all temptations and troubles: for he is among them. Now after what manner he is with them, he declareth likewise well-favouredly.

<small>What the prophet teacheth in this verse.</small>

Here thou seest, that as soon as the word of God goeth forth, and as soon as there be any that receive it, and abide by it, immediately the devil and all his angels step forth and move the world with all the power thereof against it, to put it down, and utterly to destroy them that have it and acknowledge it. For look, what our Lord God speaketh or doth, it must be tried and go through the fire. This is very needful for christian men to know; else might they fail and think thus in their minds: How standeth this together? The prophet saith afore, "The Lord is my shepherd, I shall lack nothing." And here he saith contrary, namely, that he must walk in the dark valley. And in the next verse follow-

<small>Persecution.</small>

ing he confesseth, that he hath enemies: whereby he giveth sufficiently to understand, that he lacketh many, yea, all things. For he that hath enemies, and lieth in a dark valley, seeth no light; that is to say, he hath neither comfort nor hope, but is forsaken by every man, and every thing is black and dark before his eyes, yea, even the fair clear sun. How is this true then, that he should lack nothing?

Here must thou not order thyself after thine own eyes, and follow natural reason, as doth the world, unto whom it is impossible to see this rich and glorious comfort of christian men, that they should lack nothing. Yea, certainly they hold that the contrary is true, namely, that there are no people upon earth more poor, more miserable, and more unhappy than christian men: yea, with all their diligence and courage help they thereto, that they may be most abominably persecuted, banished, shamed, and put to death: and in so doing they think they do God's service therein. It appeareth therefore outwardly, as though christian men were but sheep driven away and forsaken by God, and given over already into the wolves' mouths, and to be even such as lack nothing but altogether[1]. *We may not order ourselves after the outward sight.*

Again, they that serve that great god Mammon, or the belly, appear in the world to be those good sheep, which, as the psalm saith, lack nothing; being richly provided for by God, comforted, and preserved from all peril and misfortune. For they have their own heart's desire, honour, good, joy, pleasure, every man's favour, &c. Neither need they be afraid to be persecuted or put to death for the faith's sake. For as long as they put not their trust in Christ, the only true Shepherd, nor acknowledge him; whether they believe on the devil or his dam, or do whatsoever they will beside with covetousness, &c., they are taken not only for welldoers therein, but also for the living saints, which bide still by the old faith, and will not be deceived through heresy; which is, as David teacheth here, that the Lord only is the shepherd. So abominable and grievous mortal sin is it to believe on this shepherd, and to acknowledge him, that there came never such a sin upon earth. For even the pope's holiness, which else can dispense with all sins and forgive them, cannot remit this only crime. *The servants of Mammon.* *The pope will not forgive him that putteth his whole trust in Christ.*

[1 Perhaps for, *lack not one thing, but all together.*]

Therefore, I say, in this thing do not thou follow the world and thine own reason, which, while they judge after the outward appearance, become foolish, and hold the prophet but for a liar in that he saith, "I shall lack nothing." But, as I said afore, hold thou thee fast unto the word and promises of God; hearken unto thy shepherd, how and what he saith unto thee; and order thyself according unto his voice, not according to that which the eye seeth, or the heart feeleth: and so hast thou the victory. Thus doth the prophet: he confesseth that he walketh in the valley of the shadow of death, that is, that he is compassed about with trouble, heaviness, anguish, necessity, &c.; as thou mayest see at more large in his stories and other psalms. Item, that he hath need of comfort; whereby it is sufficiently declared, that he is in heaviness. Item, that he hath enemies; and yet he saith: Though my temptations were more and greater, and though I were in a worse case; yea, though I were in death's mouth already, yet do not I fear any misfortune. Not that I am able to help myself through mine own provision, travail, labour, or succour; neither do I trust to mine own wisdom, virtue, kingly power, and riches: for in this matter the help, counsel, comfort, and power of all men is far too little. But this is it that doth it, even that the Lord is with me. As if he would say: Certainly of mine own behalf I am feeble, in heaviness, vexed, and compassed about with all manner of peril and misfortune. My heart also and conscience is not quiet, because of my sins. I feel an horrible fearfulness of death and hell, so that I might in manner despair. But though all the world, yea, and the gates of hell be set against me, yet will I therefore not be discouraged. Yea, I will not be afraid for all the misfortune and pain that they are able to lay upon me. The Lord is with me: the Lord, I say, which made heaven and earth, and all that therein is, unto whom all creatures, angels, devils, men, sin, death, &c., are subject. Summa, he that hath all things in his own power, is my counsel-giver, my comforter, my defender, and helper. Therefore am I afraid of no misfortune.

After this manner doth Asaph speak also in the seventy-second Psalm, where he comforteth the Christian against that great stumbling-block, that the ungodly have such prosperity upon earth, and that the beloved saints of God, on the other side, are ever plagued, &c., and saith: "If I have but thee, O Lord, I pass not upon heaven nor earth. Though both body and soul should perish, yet thou, O God, art the comfort of my heart, and my portion."

Now after what manner the Lord is with him, he sheweth farthermore, and saith:

Thy staff and thy sheep-hook do comfort me.

The Lord, saith he, is with me; but not bodily, that I may see or hear him. This presence of the Lord, whereof I speak, is not comprehended with the five wits. Only faith seeth it. The same is sure, that the Lord is nigher unto us than we are to ourselves. Whereby? even by the word. Therefore saith he: "Thy staff and thy sheep-hook comfort me." As if he would say: In all my troubles and necessities I find nothing upon earth, whereby I may be helped to be at rest. Only the word of God is my staff and sheep-hook, whereby I hold me, and stand up again. And sure I am likewise by it, that the Lord is with me, and doth not only strength and comfort me by the same word in all troubles and temptations, but also delivereth me from all mine enemies, spite of the devil and the world. How the Lord is present with many faithful men.

With these words, "Thy staff and thy sheep-hook do comfort me," cometh he again unto the similitude of the shepherd and the sheep, and will say thus much: Like as a bodily shepherd ruleth his sheep with the staff or sheep-hook, and leadeth them to the pasture and to fresh water, where they find meat and drink, and defendeth them with the sheep-hook against all peril; even so doth the Lord, that true shepherd, guide and rule me with his staff, that is to say, with his word; to the intent that in his sight I should walk with a good belief and a merry conscience, and know to beware of untrue doctrine and false holiness. Besides this, he defendeth me also against all jeopardy and misfortune, bodily and spiritual, and delivereth me from all mine enemies with his staff; that is to say, with the same word doth he strength and comfort me so richly, that there is no misfortune so great, whether it be bodily or spiritual, but I am able to come out of it, and to overcome it. The similitude of the shepherd.

By this thou seest, that the prophet speaketh here of no help, defence, or comfort of man. Neither draweth he out This goeth spiritually to work.

any sword, &c. It goeth here all secretly and privily to work, even by the word: so that no man can spy this defence and comfort, but only they that believe. And here doth David write a general rule for all christian men, which is well to be noted; namely, that there is none other mean way upon earth for any man to be delivered out of all temptations, save only to cast all his burden upon God, and to hold him fast by his word of grace, to cleave surely unto it, and in no wise to suffer it to be taken from him. Whoso doth this can be content, whether he be in prosperity or adversity, whether he live or die. And, finally, he can endure, and must needs prosper against all devils, the world, and misfortune. This, methink, is a great praise of that good word of God; and a greater power is ascribed here unto it, than is the power of all angels and men. Thus doth St Paul praise it also, Rom. i.: "The gospel," saith he, "is the power of God for the salvation of all them that believe thereon."

The office of preaching.   And with this doth the prophet touch the office of preaching: for by the mouthly preaching of the word, which goeth in at the ears, and that the heart taketh hold upon by faith, and by the holy sacraments, doth our Lord God bring all this to pass in his christian congregation; namely, to the intent that the people may have faith, be strengthened in belief, and preserved in the true doctrine: item, that they may finally endure against all temptations of the devil and the world. For since the beginning of the world hath God dealt thus with all his saints by his word, and beside the same hath he given them outward tokens of grace. This I say, because that no man should take upon him without these means to meddle with God, or to choose himself a peculiar way unto heaven; else shall he fall and break his neck, as the pope and his hath done, and as the anabaptists and other seditious spirits do yet this day. And with these words, "Thy staff and thy sheep-hook do comfort me," will the prophet shew some special thing. As if he would say: Moses is a shepherd likewise, and hath also a staff and a sheep-hook: nevertheless he doth nothing else but compel and punish his sheep, and overladeth them with an untolerable burthen. Acts xv. Isai. ix. Therefore is he a fearful and a terrible shepherd, of whom the sheep are afraid, and fly from him. Nevertheless thou, Lord, with thy staff and sheep-hook compellest not thy sheep, neither makest them afraid, nor overchargest them, but giveth them comfort.

Therefore speaketh he here of the office of preaching the new Testament, whereby tiding is brought unto the world, that Christ came upon earth to save sinners, and thereby hath obtained them such a salvation, that he hath given his life for them. All they that believe this shall not perish, but have everlasting life. John iii. This is the staff and sheep-hook, whereby the souls take refreshing, comfort, and joy. Wherefore in the spiritual sheepfold, that is to say, in the kingdom of Christ, there ought none other law to be preached, but the gospel; which the prophet with ornate words calleth the staff and sheep-hook of comfort, whereby they be strengthened in faith, refreshed in their hearts, and receive consolation in all manner of troubles, and even at the point of death. *The staff and the sheep-hook.*

They that so preach use the spiritual shepherd's office aright, feed the sheep of Christ in a green meadow, lead them to the fresh water, refresh their souls, keep them that they be not deceived, and comfort them with the staff and sheep-hook of Christ, &c. And where thou hearest such a one, be sure thou hearest Christ himself. Such men also ought to be taken for true shepherds, that is to say, for the ministers of Christ and the stewards of God. Neither ought it to be regarded, that the world crieth out upon them, and calleth them heretics and deceivers. Again, they that teach any thing else contrary to the gospel, causing men to trust to their own works, merits, and to their own feigned holiness, these no doubt, though they boast never so much to be successors of the apostles, and deck themselves with the name and title of the christian church, yea, though they raised up dead men, yet are they wolves and murderers; which spare not the flock of Christ, scatter them abroad, torment them, and kill them not only spiritually, but bodily also, as men may see now before their eyes. *What they be that lead Christ's sheep in a green meadow.*

Like as the prophet here afore doth call God's word, or the gospel, grass, water, the right way, a staff, and a sheep-hook; even so afterward in the fifth verse he calleth it a table prepared, an ointment, a full cup. And this similitude of the table, ointment, and cup, doth he take out of the old *The names that the word of God hath in this psalm.*

Testament from the God's service of the Jews, and saith even in a manner the same that he had said afore, namely, that they which have the word of God are richly provided for in all points, both concerning the soul and body, save only that he speaketh it here with other figures and allegories. First, bringeth he in the similitude of the table, whereupon the shewbread lay continually. Exod. xxv. xl. And then declareth he what the same did signify, and saith:

Thou preparest a table before me against mine enemies. Thou anointest mine head with oil, and fillest my cup full.

Here doth he knowledge plainly, that he hath enemies. But he saith, he keepeth him from them, and driveth them back by this means, namely, because the Lord hath prepared a table before him against those his enemies. Is not this a wonderful defender? I would have thought he should have prepared before him a strong wall, a mighty bulwark, deep ditches, armour, and other harness and weapons, whereby he might be sure from his enemies, and discomfit them. And now cometh he and prepareth him a table, to eat and to drink on, and so to smite his enemies.

There could I be content to fight also, if the enemies might be overcome without any jeopardy, care, travail, and labour, and I too do nothing else but to sit at a table, to eat and drink and be merry.

With these words, "Thou preparest a table before me against mine enemies," will the prophet declare the great, excellent, and wonderful power of the word of God. As if he would say: Thou offerest me such kindness, O Lord, and feedest me so well and richly at thy table which thou hast prepared for me, that is, thou enduest me so plenteously with the exceeding knowledge of thy good word, so that through the same I have not only plenteous consolation inwardly in my heart, against mine own evil conscience, against fear and dread of death, and the wrath and judgment of God; but outwardly also, through the same word, I am become so valiant and so invincible a giant, that all mine enemies can bring nothing to pass against me. The more wroth, mad, and unreasonable they are against me, the less I regard it: yea, I am so much the more quiet in myself, glad, and content; and that of none other occasion, save only that I have

The great power of God's word.

thy word. The same giveth me such power and courage against all mine enemies: so that when they rage fiercely and are most mad of all, I am better content in my mind, than if I sat at a table where I might have all that my heart could desire, meat, drink, mirth, pleasure, minstrelsy, &c.

There hearest thou again, how highly this holy David magnifieth and praiseth the good word of God; namely, how that by the same they that believe overcome and win the victory against the devil, the world, the flesh, sin, a man's own conscience, and against death. For if a man have the word, and take more hold of it by faith, then must all these enemies, which else are invincible, be fain to give back and to yield themselves. And it is a marvellous victory and power, yea, and a very stout boasting of such as believe, that they subdue and overcome all these horrible, yea, and in manner almighty, enemies; not with raging, not with biting, not with resisting, not with striking again, not with taking of vengeance, not with seeking of counsel and help here and there; but with eating, drinking, pleasure, sitting, being merry, and taking of rest. Which things, as it is said afore, come all to pass through the word. For to eat and drink is called in the scripture, to believe, to take sure hold on God's word, whereout there followeth peace, joy, comfort, strength, &c. *An high commendation of God's word.*

Natural reason can give no judgment in this wonderful victory of the faithful; for here cometh the matter to pass clean contrary to the outward senses of man. The world doth alway persecute and slay the Christian, as the most hurtful people upon earth. Now when natural reason saith this, it cannot think otherwise, but that the Christian lie under; and again, that their enemies prevail and have the victory. Thus did the Jews entreat Christ, the apostles, and the faithful, and put them ever to execution. When they had slain them, or at the least banished them, then cried they, Now have we the victory; these followers that have hurt us shall now trouble us no more. Now shall we handle every thing as we will. But when they thought themselves to have been surest of all, our Lord God sent upon them the Romans, which dealt so horribly with them, that it is a terrible thing to hear. Then after certain hundred years, as for the Romans, (which throughout all the *The natural reason of man.*

empire of Rome had slain many thousand martyrs,) God rewarded them afterward, and suffered the city of Rome in a few years to be four times spoiled by the Gothics and Vandals, and finally to be burnt, destroyed, and the empire to decay. Who had now the victory? The Jews and Romans, that shed the blood of saints like water; or the poor Christians, that suffered themselves to be ordered like slaughter-sheep, and had none other harness and weapon, but the good word of God?

<small>How it goeth with the multitude of them that believe in Christ.</small>

Thus doth David declare with these words, how it goeth with the holy christian congregation, (for he speaketh not here of his own person only,) setteth her forth in her colours, and describeth her well-favouredly; namely, how that in the sight of God she is even as a pleasant green meadow, which hath plenty of grass and fresh water: that is to say, that she is the paradise and pleasant garden of God, garnished with all his gifts, and hath his unoutspeakable treasure, the holy sacraments, and that good word, wherewith he instructeth, guideth, refresheth, and comforteth his flock. But in the sight of the world hath this congregation a far other appearance, even as though she were a black dark valley, where a man can see neither pleasure nor joy, but trouble, sorrow, and adversity. For the devil with all his power setteth himself against it, for this treasure sake. Inwardly plagueth he the congregation of God with his venomous fiery darts: outwardly treadeth he her down by sects and offences. Then kindleth he also his brand upon her, even the world, which ministereth unto her all sorrow and heaviness of heart, with persecuting, slandering, blaspheming, condemning, and murdering; insomuch that it were no wonder that dear flock of Christ were utterly destroyed in the twinkling of an eye, by such great subtilty and might both of the devil and of the world. For she cannot keep herself from her enemies; they are far too strong, too deceitful, and too mighty for her. She is even as the prophet doth here describe her, an innocent, simple, and weaponless lamb, which neither will nor can do any man harm, but is alway ready, not only to do good, but also to take evil for good.

<small>How the flock of Christ winneth.</small>

How happeneth it then, that the congregation of Christ in such weakness can escape the craftiness and tyranny of the devil and the world? The Lord is her shepherd; therefore lacketh she nothing. He feedeth and refresheth her spiritually and bodily; he keepeth her in the right way; he giveth her also his staff and sheep-hook instead of a sword, which she beareth not in the hand, but in the mouth; and not only comforteth the sorrowful therewith, but driveth away the devil also and his apostles, be they never so subtle and spiteful. Besides this, the Lord hath prepared for her also a table and Easter lamb. When her enemies are very wrothful, gnash their teeth together over her, are mad, unreasonable, in a rage, and out of their wits, and take all their subtilty, power, and might to help them for to destroy her utterly; then doth the beloved Bride of Christ set her down at her Lord's table, eateth the Easter lamb, drinketh of the fresh water, is merry, and singeth: "The Lord is my shepherd, I shall lack nothing."

These are her weapons and guns, wherewith she hath hitherto smitten and overcome all her enemies; and after the same manner shall she have the victory still unto doomsday. The more also that the devil and the world doth hurt and vex her, the better is it with her. For her edifying and increase standeth in persecution, affliction, and death. Out of this occasion did one of the old fathers say: "The blood of martyrs is a seed; where one is cast, there rise an hundred up again[1]." Of this wonderful victory sing certain psalms, as the ninth, tenth, &c. *A notable saying.*

After this same manner have I also, through the grace of God, behaved myself these eighteen years: I have ever suffered mine enemies to be wroth, to threaten, to blaspheme and condemn me; to cast their heads still against me, to imagine many evil ways, and to use divers unthirsty points. I have suffered them to take wondrous great thought, how they might destroy me, and mine, yea, God's doctrine. Moreover, I have been glad and merry, (but more at one time than at another,) and not greatly regarded their raging and madness, but have holden me by the staff of comfort, and had recourse unto the Lord's table; that is, I have com- *The author of this book.*

[1 The sentiment is found in Augustine, Enarrat. in Psalm lv. (lvi.) Pars I. Opera, Tom. VIII. p. 128. C. Ed. 1541. Effusus est multus et magnus martyrum sanguis: quo effuso, tanquam seminata seges ecclesiæ fertilius pullulavit.—Compare also Enarrat. in Psalm. cxl. (cxli.) Ib. p. 354. I. Tertull. Apol. adv. Gentes, c. 50.]

mitted the cause unto God, wherein he hath so led me, that I have obtained all my will and mind. And in the mean time have I done little or nothing, but spoken unto him a *Paternoster,* or some little psalm. This is all my harness, wherewith I have defended me hitherto, not only against mine enemies; but also through the grace of God brought so much to pass, that when I look behind me, and call to remembrance, how it hath stood in the papistry, I do even wonder that the matter is come so far. I would never have thought that the tenth part should have come to pass, as it is now before our eyes. He that hath begun it shall bring it well to an end; yea, though nine hells and worlds were set on an heap together against it. Let every christian man, therefore, learn this science; namely, that he hold him by this staff and sheep-hook, and resort unto this table, when heaviness or any other misfortune is at hand. And so shall he doubtless receive strength and comfort against every thing that oppresseth him.

<small>The ointment.</small> The second similitude is of the ointment, whereof there is mention made oft-times in the holy scripture. It was some precious oil, as balm, or else some other sweet-smelling water; and the use was, to anoint the kings and priests withal. When the Jews also held their solemn feasts, and were disposed to be merry, they did anoint or sprinkle themselves with such precious ointment, as Christ declared likewise in the sixth of Matthew, where he saith: "When thou fastest, anoint thine head, and wash thy face," &c. The use then of this ointment was had among those people, when they were disposed to be merry and glad: like as the Magdalene also thought to make the Lord merry, when she poured upon his head the precious water of nardus; for she saw that he was heavy.

<small>The full cup.</small> The third similitude is of the cup, which they brought in their God's service, when they offered drink-offerings, and were merry before the Lord.

<small>The rich comfort of christian men.</small> With these words then, "Thou anointest my head with oil, and fillest my cup full," will the prophet describe the great rich comfort, which they that are faithful have by the word of God; so that their consciences are quiet, glad, and at rest in the midst of all temptations and troubles, yea, even of death. As if he would say: Doubtless the Lord maketh me a marvellous man of war, and harnesseth me

wondrously against mine enemies. I thought he should have put material harness upon me, set an helmet upon mine head, given me a sword in my hand, and have warned me to be circumspect, and to take diligent heed to my matter, lest mine enemies should overtake me. Now cometh he and setteth me down at a table, and prepareth me a goodly banquet, anointeth mine head with precious balm: or, after the manner of our country, setteth a garland upon mine head, as if I should go to some pastime or dancing, and not fight with mine enemies; and to the intent that there should be no scarceness, he filleth my cup full, that I may drink, make good cheer, and be drunken. The table then prepared is my harness, the precious ointment is my helmet, and the full cup is my sword. With these do I overcome all mine enemies. Is not this a marvellous preparing to war, and yet a more wonderful victory? Thus will he say: Lord, thy guests which sit at thy table, that is to say, the faithful, shall not only be strong and valiant giants against all their enemies, but they shall be merry also and drunken. For why? thou makest them good cheer, *Spiritual drunkenness.* as a rich host useth to do to his guests; thou feedest them well, thou makest them lusty and glad, thou fillest into them so much, that they must needs be drunken. This is all done by the word of grace. For by the same doth the Lord our shepherd feed and strength so the hearts of his faithful, that they dare defy all their enemies, and say with the prophet, "I am not afraid for thousands of the people, that compass me around about." Psalm iii. And here afore in the fourth verse: "I fear no evil; for thou, Lord, art with me." With this, yea, even through the same word, doth he give them also the Holy Ghost, which maketh them not only to take good stomachs unto them, and to be of good courage, but so quiet also in themselves and merry, that for the same great exceeding joy they are even drunken.

He speaketh here then of a spiritual strength, of a spi- *This must be spiritually understand.* ritual drunkenness, which is a godly strength, Rom. i.; "a joy," as St Paul calleth it, "in the Holy Ghost," Rom. xiv.; and a blessed drunkenness, when people are not full of wine, whereout followeth inconvenience, but full of the Holy Ghost. Ephes. v. This is the harness and the weapons, wherewith our Lord God prepareth his faithful against the devil and the world; namely, in their mouth giveth he them his word, and in their heart he giveth courage, that is to say, the Holy Ghost. With such ordnance put they from them all fear, and with gladness buckle they with all their enemies, smite them and overcome them with all their might, wisdom, and holiness.

Such soldiers were the apostles on Whit-Sunday, when they went up to Jerusalem against the commandment of the emperor and the high priests, and ordered themselves, as if they had been very gods, and all the other but grasshoppers, and went even through with all power and joy, as if they had been drunken; insomuch that some had them in derision therefore, and said, They were "full of sweet wine." Nevertheless St Peter declared out of the prophet Joel, that they were not full of sweet wine, but full of the Holy Ghost. And so he smote about him with his sword, that is, he opened his mouth, and preached the word of God, and felled down three thousand souls at once from the power of the devil. Acts ii.

This strength, joy, and blessed drunkenness doth not only shew itself in the faithful, when they be in prosperity, and have peace; but also when they suffer and die. As when the council at Jerusalem caused the apostles to be beaten, they were glad of it, that they were worthy to suffer rebuke for the name of Christ. Acts v. And in the fifth to the Romans doth St Paul say: "We rejoice also in troubles," &c. *The stedfast and joyful hearts of them that have suffered death for the word of God.* Afterward were there many martyrs also, which with merry hearts and laughing mouths went unto their death, as if they had gone to some pastime or dance. Like as we read of St Agnes and St Agatha, which were virgins of thirteen or fourteen years old[1], and of other more, which were of such inward courage and confidence, that they did not only overcome the devil and the world by their death, but also made good cheer even then with their hearts, as though they had been drunken of very joy. And this grieveth the devil exceeding sore, namely, when men are

[[1] Some account of these persons, together with the hymns composed to their memory, may be found in Daniel's Hymnologus Christianus, Vol. I. p. 945. Ed. 1841. See also Nichols on the Common Prayer.]

at such quietness in themselves, that they despise his great might and guile. In our time also have there been many, which for the knowledge of Christ have been glad to suffer death. We see moreover, that there be many, which with perfect understanding and faith die upon their beds, and say with Simeon, "Lord, now lettest thou thy servant depart in peace," &c., that is to a joy to behold them; of whom I have seen many myself. And all this cometh because that, as the prophet saith, they be anointed with the oil, which the forty-fourth Psalm calleth the oil of gladness; [Psal. xlv.] and because they have drunk of the full cup, which the Lord hath filled.

Yea, but thou wilt say, I feel not myself yet so apt, Objection. that I could be content to die, &c. That maketh no matter. David also, as it is said afore, hath not been sure of that Answer. science at all hours, but sometime complained, that he was cast out of God's sight. Other holy men also have not always had an hearty confidence toward God, and a perpetual delight and patience in their troubles and temptations. Note this well. St Paul sometime is so sure and certain in himself, and maketh such boast of Christ, that he careth not the curse of the law, for sin, death, nor for the devil. "I live not now," saith he, Gal. ii., "but Christ liveth in me." Item, "I desire to be loosed and to be with Christ." Phil. i. Item, "Who shall separate us from the love of God, which spared not his own Son, but hath given him for us all? How shall he not with him give us all things also? Shall trouble, anguish, persecution, sword, &c., separate us from him?" Rom. viii. There speaketh he of death, of the devil, and of all evil with such a courage, as if he were the strongest and greatest of all saints, unto whom death were but a sport. But incontinently in another place he speaketh, as though he were the weakest and greatest sinner upon earth. 1 Cor. ii. "I was with you," saith he, "in weakness, in fear, and in much trembling." "I am carnal, sold under sin, which is in my members. O wretched man that I am! who shall deliver me from the body of this death?" Rom. vii. And in the fifth to the Galatians he teacheth, that in the saints of God there is a continual strife of the flesh against the spirit, &c. Therefore oughtest thou not immediately to despair, though thou feelest thyself feeble and faint-hearted: and pray diligently, that thou mayest endure by the word, and increase in the faith and knowledge of Christ; as the prophet doth here, and teacheth other men likewise so to do, and saith: "Oh let thy lovingkindness and mercy follow me all the days of my life, that I may dwell in the house of the Lord for ever."

Forasmuch as the devil never ceaseth to plague the faithful inwardly with deceitfulness of false teachers, and with the violence of tyrants, he prayeth here therefore at the end earnestly, that God, which hath given him this treasure, will keep him fast by it also unto the end, and saith: "O gracious God, shew me such favour, that thy lovingkindness and mercy may follow me all the days of my life." And immediately he declareth, what he calleth this lovingkindness and mercy, namely, that he may remain in the house of the Lord for ever. As if he would say: Thou hast begun the matter; thou hast given me thy holy word, and accepted me among them that are thy people, which do knowledge, praise, and give thanks unto thee: grant me, therefore, such grace from henceforth, that I may continue still by the same word, and never to be separated more from thy holy christian flock. Thus doth he pray also in the twenty-sixth Psalm: "One thing," saith he, "have I desired of the Lord, which I would fain have; namely, that I may dwell in the house of the Lord all the days of my life, to behold the fair beauty of the Lord," that is to say, the true service of God, "and to visit his temple."

<small>Why the prophet maketh this prayer.</small>

<small>[Psal. xxvii.]</small>

<small>A notable ensample.</small>

The prophet then here, by his ensample, teacheth and exhorteth all such as put their trust in God, that they be not careless, proud, or presumptuous in themselves; but to fear and give themselves unto prayer, that they lose not this treasure. And doubtless this earnest exhortation should tear us up, and make us fervent unto diligent prayer. For seeing that holy David, which was a prophet, so highly endued with all manner of godly wisdom and knowledge, and with divers great excellent gifts of God, seeing he, I say, did pray so oft and with such great earnest, that he might abide by this treasure; much more shall it be meet for us, which are utterly nothing to be compared unto him, and live also now at the end of the world, when, as Christ and the apostles say, it shall be an horrible and perilous time; it shall be much more convenient, I say, to watch and pray with all earnest and diligence, that we may continue in the house of the Lord all the days of our life; namely, that we may hear the word of God, and receive the manifold commodities and fruits that come of it, as it is rehearsed afore, and continue in the same unto the end. Which grant us Christ, our only Shepherd and Saviour! Amen.

<small>We have most need to watch and pray.</small>

  Imprinted in Southwark by James Nycolson, for
     John Gough.

    Cum privilegio.

AN EXHORTATION

TO THE

CARRYING OF CHRIST'S CROSS.

An Exhor
tation to the carienge of Chrystes crosse wyth a true and brefe confutation of false and papisticall doctryne.

2 Timo. 3.

All, that wyll lyue godly in Chryste Jesu must suffer persecucyon.

THE CONTENTS OF THIS BOOK

AS THEY FOLLOW IN EVERY CHAPTER.

CHAPTER		PAGE
	The Preface to the christian reader	[62]
I.	What we be, and where we be	[63]
II.	Persecution must not be strange unto us	[65]
III.	Trouble cannot hurt God's children	[67]
IV.	The cross is commodious and profitable	[71]
V.	How the papists hold their four special articles, which they so grievously persecute for	[80]
VI.	How God's word teacheth of the supper, with confutation of transubstantiation	[82]
VII.	How God's word teacheth of Christ's sacrifice, with the Romish blasphemy therein reproved	[88]
VIII.	Of praying for the dead, the true doctrine	[90]
IX.	Of praying to saints	[92]
X.	The Romish doctrine of the sacrament confuted more largely	[93]
XI.	The popish doctrine of the sacrifice in massing confuted	[96]
XII.	The confutation of the papists' sacrificing and praying for the dead	[101]
XIII.	The confutation of the heresy of praying to saints departed out of this world	[104]
XIV.	The knitting up of the matter, and conclusion or peroration, with prayer for the help of God in this time of danger and divers temptations	[107]

AN EXHORTATION

TO THE

CARRYING OF CHRIST'S CROSS.

THE HOLY SPIRIT OF GOD, WHICH IS HIS EARNEST PLEDGE GIVEN TO HIS PEOPLE FOR THEIR COMFORT AND CONSOLATION, BE POURED INTO OUR HEARTS BY THE MIGHTY POWER AND MERITS OF OUR ALONE SAVIOUR JESUS CHRIST, NOW AND FOR EVER. AMEN.

BECAUSE I perceive plainly, that unto the evils fallen upon us which profess Christ's gospel greater are most like to ensue, and after them greater, till the measure of iniquity be upheaped, (except we shrink, and having put our hand to the plough, do look back, and so with Lot's wife fall into God's heavy displeasure incurably, all which God forbid!) and because I am persuaded of you, my dearly beloved brethren and sisters throughout the realm of England, which have professed unfeignedly the gospel of our Lord and Saviour Jesus Christ, (for unto such do I write this Epistle or Book,) how that, as you have begun to take part with God's gospel and truth, so through his grace ye will persevere and go on forwards, notwithstanding the storms risen and to arise; I cannot but write some things unto you, to encourage you to go on lustily in the way of the Lord, and not to become faint-hearted or fearful persons, whose place St John appointed with unbelievers, murderers, and idolaters in eternal perdition; but cheerfully to take the Lord's cup and drink of it, afore it draw towards the dregs and bottom; whereof at length they shall drink with the wicked to eternal destruction, which will not receive it at the first with God's children, with whom God beginneth his judgment; that, as the wicked world rejoiceth when they lament, so they may rejoice when the wicked world shall mourn, and without end feel woe intolerable.

Gen. ix.
Luke ix.

Rev. xxi.

Psal. lxxv.

1 Pet. iv.
John xvi.

CHAPTER I.

WHAT WE BE, AND WHERE WE BE.

FIRST, therefore, my dearly beloved in the Lord, I beseech you to consider, that though ye be in the world, yet you are not of the world. You are not of them which look for their portion in this life, whose captain is the god of this world, even Satan, who now ruffleth it apace, as he were wood, because his time on earth is not long. But you are of them which look for a city of God's own building. You are of them which know themselves to be here but pilgrims and strangers; for here you have no dwelling-place. You are of them whose portion is the Lord, and which have their hope in heaven; whose captain is Christ Jesus, the Son of God, and governor of heaven and earth. Unto him is given all power; yea, he is God Almighty with the Father and the Holy Ghost, praise-worthy for ever. You are not of them which receive the beast's mark; which here rejoice, laugh, and have their heart's ease, joy, paradise, and pleasure: but you are of them which have received the angel's mark, yea, God's mark; which here lament, mourn, sigh, sob, and have your wilderness to wander in, your purgatory, and even hell. You are not of them which cry, Let us eat and drink, for to-morrow we shall die. You are not of that number which say, they have made a covenant with death and hell for hurting them. You are not of them, which take it but for a vain thing to serve the Lord. You are not of them which are lulled and rocked asleep in Jezebel's bed, a bed of security. You are not in the number of them that say, Tush, God is in heaven and seeth us not, nor much passeth what we do. You are not of the number of them which will fall down for the muck of the world, to worship the fiend, or for displeasing of men to worship the golden image. Finally, you are not of the number of them which set more by their pigs, than by Christ; which for ease and rest in this life will say and do as Antiochus biddeth them do or say; and will follow the multitude to do evil with Zedekiah and the three hundred false prophets; yea, Achab, Jezebel, and the whole court and country.

John xiv.
Psal. xvii.
2 Cor. iv.
Rev. xii.
Heb. xi.
1 Pet. ii.
Heb. xiii.
Psal. xvi. cxix.
Matt. xxviii. Rom. ix.
1 John v. Rev. xiii. Luke vi.
Ezek. ix. Matt. v.
Isai. xxii.
1 Cor. xv.
Isai. xxviii.
Mal. iii.
[Rev. ii. 22.]
Ezek. viii. Psal. lxxiii.
Luke iv.
Dan. iii.
Matt. viii. Luke v.
1 Mac. i. ii.
Prov. xxiii.
1 Kings xxii.

But you be of the number of them which are dead already, or at least in dying daily to yourselves and to the world. You are of them which have made a covenant with God to forsake themselves and Satan in this world. You are of them which say, Nay, the Lord hath all things written in his memorial book for such as fear him and remember his name. You are of them which have their loins girded about, and their lights burning in their hands, like unto men that wait for their Lord's coming. You are in the number of them that say, The Lord looketh down from heaven and beholdeth all the children of men, from the habitation of his dwelling he considereth all them that dwell upon the earth. You are of them which will worship the only Lord God, and will not worship the works of man's hands, though the oven burn never so hot. You are in the number of them, to whom Christ is precious and dear; which cry out rather, because your habitation is prolonged here, as David did, which Mattathias followed, and the godly Jews, which knew the way to life to be a strait way, and few to go through it; which will not stick to follow poor Micheas, although he be racked and cast into prison, having the sun, moon, and seven stars, and all against him.

<small>Rom. vi. Coloss. iii.</small>
<small>Mal. iii.</small>
<small>Luke xii.</small>
<small>Psal. xiv. xxxiii. ci.</small>
<small>Deut. vi. Matt. ix. Dan. iii.</small>
<small>1 Pet. ii.</small>
<small>Psal. cxx.</small>
<small>1 Mac. ii.</small>
<small>Matt. vii.</small>
<small>1 Kings xxii.</small>

Thus, therefore, dearly beloved, remember first that, as I said, you are not of this world; Satan is not your captain, your joy and paradise is not here, your companions are not the multitude of worldlings, and such as seek to please men and to live here at ease in the service of Satan. But you are of another world: Christ is your captain; your joy is in heaven, where your conversation and civility[1] is; your companions are the fathers, patriarchs, prophets, apostles, martyrs, virgins, confessors, and the dear saints of God, which followed the Lamb whithersoever he went, dipping their garments in his blood; knowing this life and world to be full of evil, a warfare, a smoke, a shadow, a vapour, and as replenished, so environed with all kind of miseries.

<small>Phil. iii. Heb. xiii.</small>
<small>Rev. vii.</small>
<small>Job vii. viii. xiv. Psal. xc. cii. James iv.</small>

[1 Civility: citizenship.]

CHAPTER II.

PERSECUTION IS NOT STRANGE.

THIS is the first thing I would give you often and diligently with yourselves to consider and muse upon, namely, what you be, and where you be. Then, secondarily, forget not to call to mind, that you ought not to think it any strange thing, if misery, trouble, adversity, persecution, and displea- _{1 Pet. iv.} sure come upon you. For how can it otherwise be, but that trouble and persecution must come upon you? Can the _{John xiv.} world love you, which are none of his? Worldly men are the soldiers of your chief enemy, and can they regard you? Can Satan suffer you to be in rest, which will not do him _{1 Pet. v.} homage? Can this way be easy, which of itself is strait? _{Matt. vii.} Will you look to travel, and have no foul way, nor rain? Will shipmen shrink, or sailors of the sea, if storms arise? Do they not look for such?

And, dearly beloved, did not we enter into God's ship _{1 Pet. iii.} and ark of baptism at the first? Will you then count it strange, if perils and tempests blow? Are not you travelling to your heavenly city of Jerusalem, where is all joy and felicity? and will you now tarry by the way for storms or showers? The mart and fair will then be past; the night _{John ix.} will fall; ye cannot travel; the door will be sparred, and _{Matt. xxv.} the bride will be at supper. Therefore away with dainty niceness. Will you think the Father of heaven will deal more gently with you in this age, than he hath done with other his dearest friends in other[2] ages? What way and weather, what storms and tempests, what disease, trouble, and disquietness found Abel, Noe, Abraham, Isaac, Jacob, _{Gen. iv. vi.} and good Joseph! Which of these had so fair a life and _{vii. viii. xi. &c.} restful times as we have had? Moses, Aaron, Samuel, David the king, and all the good kings, priests, and prophets in the old Testament, at one time or another, if not throughout their life, did feel a thousand parts more misery than we have felt hitherto. As for the new Testament, Lord God, how great was the affliction of Mary, Joseph, Zachary, Eli- _{Matt. ii.} zabeth, John the Baptist, than whom among the children of

[2 Old edition, *our*.]

men none arose greater, of all the apostles and evangelists; yea, of Jesus Christ our Lord, the dear Son and dearling of God! And since the time of the apostles, how many and great are the martyrs, confessors, and such as suffered the shedding of their blood in this life, rather than they would be stained in their journey, or lodge in any of Satan's inns, so that the storms or winds which fell in their travellings might not touch them. Wherefore, dearly beloved, let us think, what we are, and how far meet to be matched with these, whom yet we look to be placed in heaven.

<small>Eusebius, Eccles. Hist. Tripart. Historia.</small>

But with what face can we look for this, that are so fearful, unwilling, and backward to leave that which, will we, nill we, we must leave, and that so shortly, as we know not the time when? Where is our abrenouncing and forsaking of the world and the flesh, which we solemnly sware in baptism? Ah, shameless cowards that we be! which will not follow the trace of so many fathers, patriarchs, kings, priests, prophets, apostles, evangelists, and saints of God, yea, even of the very Son of God. How many now go with you lustily, as I and all your brethren in bonds and exile for the gospel? Pray for us; for, God willing, we will not leave you now, we will go before you. You shall see in us, that we preached no lies nor tales of tubs; but even the very true word of God, for which we, by God's grace and help of your prayers, will willingly and joyfully give our blood to be shed for the confirmation of the same, as already we have given liberally our goods, living, friends, and natural country. For now we are certain, that we be in the high way to heaven's bliss; as Paul saith, "By many tribulations and persecutions we must enter into God's kingdom." And because we would go thither ourselves, and bring you thither also, therefore the devil stirreth up the coals. And forasmuch as we all loitered in the way, he therefore hath received power of God to overcast the weather and to stir up storms, that we, God's children, might go faster, making more speed and haste to go on forwards. As for counterfeits and hypocrites, they will tarry and linger till the storm be past. And so when they come, the market will be done, and the doors sparred, it is to be feared. Read Matthew xxv. This wind will blow God's children forward, and the devil's darlings backward. Therefore, like God's children, let us go on for-

<small>2 Pet. i.</small>

ward apace; the wind is on our back, hoist up the sails, lift up your hearts and hands unto God in prayer, and keep your anchor of faith to cast in time on the rock of God's word, and in his mercy in Christ; and I warrant you. Heb. vi.

And thus much for you, secondly, to consider, that affliction, persecution, and trouble is no strange thing to God's children; and therefore it should not dismay, discourage, or discomfort us, being none other thing than all God's dear friends have tasted in their journey to heavenward. As I would in this troublesome time, that ye should consider what you be by the goodness of God in Christ, even citizens of heaven, though you be presently in the flesh, even in a strange region, on every side full of fierce enemies, and what weather and way the dearest friends of God have found; even so would I have you, thirdly, to consider for your further comfort, that if you shrink not, but go on forward pressing to the mark appointed, all the power of your enemies shall not overcome you, neither in any point hurt you.

CHAPTER III.

TROUBLE CANNOT HURT GOD'S CHILDREN.

But this must you not consider according to the judgment of reason and her sense, but after the judgment of God's word and the experience of faith; else you mar all. For to reason and experience or sense of the outward man we poor souls, which stick to God's word to serve him as he requireth only, are counted to be vanquished and overcome, in that we are cast into prison, lose our livings, friends, goods, country, and life also at length concerning this world. But, dearly beloved, God's word teacheth otherwise, and faith falleth accordingly. Is it not written, "Who shall separate us from the love of God? shall tribulation, or anguish, or persecution, either hunger, either nakedness, either peril, either sword? As it is written, For thy sake are we killed all day long, and be counted as sheep appointed to be slain. Nevertheless in all these things we overcome through him that loved us. For I am sure that Rom. viii. Psal. xliv.

neither death, neither life, neither angels, nor rule, neither power, neither things present, neither things to come, neither height, nor loweth, neither any other creature, shall be able to part us from that love, wherewith God loveth us in Christ Jesus our Lord." This spake one, which was in affliction, as I am, for the Lord's gospel's sake; his holy name be praised therefore, and he grant me grace with the same to continue in like suffering unto the end! This, I say, one spake, which was in affliction for the gospel; but yet so far from being overcome, that he rejoiced rather of the victory which the gospel had. For though he was bound, the gospel was not bound; and therefore rendered he thanks unto God, who always giveth victory in Christ, and openeth the savour of his knowledge by us and such as suffer for his truth; although they shut us up never so much, and drive us never so far out of our natural country in every place.

2 Tim. ii.

2 Cor. ii.

The world for a time may deceive itself, aye thinking it hath the victory; but yet the end will try the contrary. Did not Cain think he had the victory, when Abel was slain? But how say ye now? Is it not found otherwise? Thought not the old world that they were wise and well, and Noe a fool, which would creep into an ark, leaving his house, lands, and possessions? For I think he was in an honest state. As for the world, they judged that he was a dastard and a fool: but I pray you, who was wise when the flood came? Abraham, I trow, was counted a fool to leave his own country and friends, kith and kin, because of God's word. But, dearly beloved, we know it proved otherwise. I will leave all the patriarchs, and come to Moses and the children of Israel. Tell me, were they not thought to be overcome, and stark mad, when for fear of Pharao, at God's word, they ran into the Red Sea? Did not Pharao and the Egyptians think themselves sure of the victory? But, I trow, it proved clean contrary. Saul was thought to be well, and David in evil case and most miserable, because he had no hole to hide him in; but yet at length Saul's misery was seen, and David's felicity began to appear. The prophet Michaias, being cast into prison for telling Achab the truth, was thought overcome of Zedechias and other false prophets: but, my good brethren, and sisters, the holy history telleth otherwise. Who did not think the prophets unhappy in

Gen. iv.

Gen. vii. viii.

Gen. xii.

Exod. xiv.

1 Sam. xvi. &c.

1 Kings xxii.

Jer. xx.

their time? for they were slain, imprisoned, laughed to scorn, and jested at of every man. And so were all the apostles; yea, the dearly beloved friend of God, John the Baptist, who was beheaded, and that in prison, even at a dancing damsel's desire. As all these, to the judgment of reason, were then counted heretics, runagates, unlearned, fools, fishers, publicans, &c., so now unhappy and overcome in deed, if God's word and faith did not shew the contrary. *1 Cor. iv.*

But what speak I of those? Look upon Jesus Christ; to whom we must be fashioned here, if we will be like him elsewhere. How say you, was he not taken for almost a fool, a seditious person, a new fellow, an heretic, and one overcome of every body, even forsaken both of God and men? But the end told them and telleth us another tale; for now is he in majesty and glory joyful. When he was led to Pilate or Herod, or when he was in prison in Caiphas' house, did not their reason think that he was overcome? When he was beaten, buffeted, scourged, crowned with thorns, hanged upon the cross, and utterly left by all his disciples, taunted by the high priests and holy fathers, cursed by the commons, railed on by the magistrates, and laughed to scorn by the lewd heathen; would not a man then have thought, that he had been out of the way, and his disciples to follow and believe him? Think you, the whilst he lay in his grave, men did not point with their fingers, when they saw any that had loved and believed in him and his doctrine, saying, Where is their master and teacher now? What! is he gone? Forsooth, if they had not been fools, they might well have known this learning he taught could not long continue. Our doctors and Pharisees are no fools, now they may see. On this sort men either spake or might have spoken against all such as loved Christ or his doctrine: but yet they and all such were proved fools and wicked wretches. For our Saviour arose despite their beards, and published his gospel plentifully, in spite of their heads and the heads of all the wicked world, with the great powers of the same; always overcoming, and then most of all, when he and his doctrine was thought to have the greatest fall. *Rom. viii.*

Now, dearly beloved, the wicked world rejoiceth, the papists are puffed up against poor Christ and his people:

after their old kind now cry they, Where are these new-found preachers? Are they not in the Tower, Marshalsea, in the Fleet, in Newgate, &c., and beyond the seas? Who would have thought that our old bishops, doctors, and deans were fools, as they would have made us believe, and indeed have persuaded some already, which are not of the wisest, specially if they come not home again to the holy church? These and such like words they have to cast in our teeth, as triumphers and conquerors. But, dearly beloved, short is their joy. They beguile themselves; this is but a lightning before their death. As God, after he had given the wicked Jews a time to repent, visited them by Vespasian and Titus most horribly, to their utter subversion, delivering first of all his people from among them; even so, my dear brethren, will he do with this age. When he hath tried his children from amongst them, as now he beginneth, and by suffering hath made us like to his Christ, and by being overcome to overcome indeed to our eternal comfort; then will he, if not otherwise, come himself in the clouds: I mean, our dear Lord, whom we confess, preach, and believe on. He will come, I say, with the blast of a trump and shout of an archangel, and so shall we be caught up in the clouds to meet him in the air; the angels gathering together the wicked wretches, which now welter and wallow, as the world and wind bloweth, to be tied in bundles, and cast into the fire which burneth for ever most painfully. There and then shall they see, who hath the victory, they or we. When they shall see us afar off in Abraham's bosom, then will they say, Alas! we thought these folks fools, and had them in derision; we thought their life madness, and their end to be without honour. But lo! how are they counted among the children of God, and their portion is with the saints. Alas! we have gone amiss, and would not hearken. Such words as these shall the wicked say one day in hell, though now they triumph as conquerors.

Eusebius, Eccles. Hist. Lib. III. cap. 5, 6, 7, 8, 9.

1 Thess. iv.

Matt. iii.

Luke xvi.

[Wisd. v.]

And thus much for you, thirdly, to look often upon; namely, that whatsover is done unto you, yea, even very death, shall not baffle or hurt you no more than it did Abel, David, Daniel, John the Baptist, Jesus Christ our Lord, with other the dear saints of God, which have suffered for his name's sake. Let not, therefore, reason be judge in this matter, but faith and God's word; in the which, if we set before our eyes the shortness of this present time wherein we suffer, and consider the eternity to come, we shall find it most certain that our enemies and persecutors shall be helpless in intolerable pains, and we, if we persevere unto the end, shall be dangerless in such felicity and joy, as the very heart of man in no point is able to conceive. Considering this, I say, we cannot but even contemn and set nothing by the sorrows and griefs of the cross, and lustily go through thick and thin with good courage. *The time of suffering is but a trifle.* *1 Cor. ii. Isai. lxiv.*

Now have I declared unto you three things necessary to be much mused upon by every one, which will abide in Christ and his gospel in these troublesome times, as I trust you all will: namely, first, to consider, that we are not of this world, nor of the number of the worldlings, nor any retainer to Satan; that we are not at home in our own country, but of another world, of the congregation of the saints and retainers to Christ, although as yet in a region replete and full of untractable enemies. Secondly, that we may not think it a strange thing to be persecuted for God's gospel, from the which the dearest friends of God were in no age free; as indeed it is impossible they should be any long time, their enemies being always about them, to destroy them if they could. And thirdly, that the assaults of our enemies, be they never so many and fierce, shall in no point be able to prevail against our faith, albeit to reason it seemeth otherwise; wherethrough we ought to conceive a good courage and comfort: for who will be afraid, when he knoweth that the enemies cannot prevail? *Heb. xii.*

CHAPTER IV.

THE CROSS IS COMMODIOUS AND PROFITABLE.

FURTHERMORE, for the more encouraging of you unto the cross, I will give you a fourth memorandum, namely, of the commodities and profits which come by the trouble and affliction now risen, and hereafter to arise, unto us which be God's children, elect through Jesus Christ. But here ye may not look to have [from] me a rehearsal of all the commodities which come by the cross to such as are well exercised therein; for that were more than I can do. I will only speak of a few; thereby to occasion you to gather, and at the length to feel and perceive more.

<small>The first commodity of the cross.</small>

<small>Amos iii.
Matt. x.
Isai. xlv.
Psalm cxlv.</small>

First, there is no cross which cometh upon any of us without the counsel of our heavenly Father. As for the fancy of fortune, it is wicked, as many places of scripture do teach. We must needs, to the commendation of God's justice, who in all things is righteous, acknowledge in ourselves that we have deserved of the hands of our heavenly Father this his cross and rod, now fallen upon us. We have deserved it, if not by our own unthankfulness, sloth, negligence, intemperance, and our sins done often by us, (whereof our consciences can and will accuse us, if we call them to council, with the examination of our former life;) yet at least by our original and birth sin, as by doubting of the greatness of God's anger and mercy, by self-love, concupiscence, and

<small>Psalm li.
Heb. xii.</small>

such like sins, which as we brought with us into this world, so do the same ever abide in us, and, even as a spring, they alway bring forth something in act with us, notwithstanding

<small>Gal v.</small>

the fight of God's good Spirit in us against it. The first commodity, therefore, that the cross bringeth, is knowledge,

<small>Psalm v.</small>

and that double, of God, and of ourselves: of God, that he

<small>Psalm li.</small>

is just, pure, and hateth sin; of ourselves, that we are born

<small>Gen. viii.
Jer. xvii.
Ephes. ii.
1 Kings viii.</small>

in sin, and from top to toe defiled with concupiscence and corruption, out of the which have sprung all the evil that ever at any time we have spoken and done. The greatest and most special whereof we are by the cross occasioned to

<small>Gen. xlii.</small>

call to mind, as did the brethren of Joseph their evil fact against him, when the cross once came upon them. And so by it we come to the surest step to get health for our souls; that is, we are driven to know our sins, original and actual, by God's justice declared in the cross.

<small>The second commodity of the cross.</small>

Secondly, the end, wherefore God declareth his justice against our sin original and actual, and would have us by his cross to consider the same, and to call to mind our former evil deeds; the end thereof, I say, is this, namely, that we may lament, be sorry, sigh, and pray for pardon; to the intent, that so doing we might obtain and have the same by the means of faith in the merits of Jesus Christ his dear Son; and that we, being humbled because of the evil that dwelleth in us, might also become thankful for God's goodness, living in continual vigilance and wariness, and suppressing the evil which liveth in us, that it bring not forth fruit unto death at any time. This second commodity of the cross, therefore, must not we count to be only a knowledge, but also a great gain of God's mercy with wonderful rich and precious virtues of faith, repentance, remission of sins, humility, thankfulness, mortification, and diligence in doing good. Not that properly the cross worketh these things of itself; but because the cross is the mean and way by the which God worketh the knowledge and feeling of these things in his children: as many both testimonies, and also ensamples in scripture, are easily found of them that diligently weigh what they hear or read therein. James i.
Note.

To these two commodities of the cross join this third, of God's singular wisdom, that it may be coupled with his justice and mercy. On this sort let us overcome it. When we see the gospel of God and his church persecuted and troubled, as now it is with us, thus, I say, let us receive the matter; namely, that because the great learned and wise men of the world use not their wisdom to love and serve God, as to natural reason he openeth himself manifestly in his visible creatures, therefore doth God justly infatuate them, and maketh them foolish, giving them up to insensibleness, especially herein. For concerning the affliction which cometh for the gospel upon the gospellers, they reason on this manner. If this were God's word, say they, if this people were God's children, surely God would then bless and prosper them and their doctrine. But now in that there is no doctrine so much hated, no people so much persecuted as they be, therefore it cannot be of God. This is of God, which our queen and old bishops have professed. For how hath God prospered and kept them! What a notable victory hath God given to her; whereas else it was impossible that things so should have come to pass, as they have done! And did not the great captain confess his fault, that he was out of the way, and not of the faith which these gospellers profess[1]? How many are come again from that which they professed to be God's word! The third commodity of the cross.

Rom. i.

Man's reason concerning the affliction of the church.

Success.

The book of North.
The relenting of many.

[1 Allusion is here made to the duke of Northumberland. An account of the circumstances mentioned may be found in Strype's Life of archbishop Cranmer, Book III. chap. iii. pp. 450—4. Ed. Oxf.]

MYLES COVERDALE

Plagues.The most part of this realm, notwithstanding the diligence of preachers to persuade them concerning this new learning which now is persecuted, never consented to it in heart, as experience teacheth. And what plagues have come upon this realm since this gospel, as they call it, came in amongst us! Afore we had plenty; but now there is nothing like as was.

Parliament. But, to let this pass, all the houses of the parliament have overthrown the laws made for the stablishing of the gospel, and new laws are erected for the continuance of that which is contrary, and was had before. All these things do teach plainly, that this their doctrine is not God's word.

Thus reason the worldly-wise, which see not God's wisdom.

The cause of our persecution. For else, if they considered that there was with us unthankfulness, no amendment of life, but all kind of contempt of God, all kind of shameless sinning against the preaching of the gospel, they must needs see that God could not but

Rev. xx. chastise and correct; and that, as he let Satan loose after he had bound him a certain time, so for men's unthankfulness, and to punish the same, he hath let those champions of Satan run abroad to plague us by them. Great was God's anger

1 Kings xx. against Ahab because he saved Benadad the king of Syria, when he had given him into his hands; and afterwards it turned to his own destruction. God would that double sorrow should have been repaid unto them, because of the sorrow that they did to the saints of God. Read Rev. xviii. As to

Causes of victory. the victory given to the queen's highness, if men had any godly wit, they might see many things in it. First, that God hath done it to win her heart with kindness unto his gospel; and as well because that they which went against her, put their trust in horses and power of men, and not in God, as because in their doctrine they sought not the propagation of God's gospel. Which thing is easily now seen by the confession of the captain; his heart loved popery, and hated the gospel. Besides this, men may easily see he was purposed never to have furthered the gospel, but so to have handled the livings of ministers, that there should never have been any minister in manner hereafter. And what one of the councillors, which would have been taken as gospellers in one of our good king's days, declare now that even they loved the gospel? Therefore no marvel why God fought against them. They were hypocrites, and under the cloke of the gospel would have debarred the queen's highness of her right. But God would not so cloke them.

Now for the relenting, returning, and recanting of some from that which they have once professed or preached, alas! who would wonder at it? For they never came to the gospel, but for commodity or gain's sake; and now for gain leave it. The multitude is no good argument to move a wise man. For who knoweth not more to love this world better than heaven; themselves better than their neighbours? "Wide is the gate," saith Christ, "and broad is the way that leadeth to destruction, and many there be which go in thereat. But strait is the gate, and narrow is the way which leadeth unto life, and few there be that find it." All the whole multitude cried out upon Jesus, Crucify him, truss him up; but I trow they were not the better part, although they were the bigger. All Chaldeans followed still their false gods; only Abraham followed the true God. And whereas they say that greater plagues are fallen on the realm in poverty and such gear than afore, it is no argument to move others than such as love their swine better than Christ. For the devil chiefly desireth his seat to be in religion. If it be there, then will he meddle with nothing that we have; all shall be quiet enough: but if he be raised there, then will he beg leave to have at our pigs. As long as with us he had the ruling of religion, which now he hath gotten again, then was he a Robin Goodfellow; he would do no hurt: but when he was tumbled out of his throne by the preaching of the gospel, then steered he about as he hath done. Notwithstanding, to be short, surely effectual he hath not been, but in the children of unbelief: them indeed he hath stirred up to be covetous, oppressors, blasphemers, usurers, whoremongers, thieves, murderers, tyrants.

And yet perchance he suffered them to profess the gospel, the more thereby to hinder it, and cause it to be slandered. How many do now appear to be true gospellers? As for the parliament and statutes thereof, no man of wisdom can think otherwise, but that look what the rulers will, the same must there be enacted. For it goeth not in those houses by the better part, but by the bigger part. It is a common saying, and no less true, *Major pars vincit meliorem;* the greater part overcometh the better. So they did in con-

Why many relent and recant.

The greater sort.

Matt. vii.

Gen. xii.

Plagues.

Matt. viii.

The parliament.

John vii.

demning Christ; Nicodemus' counsel not being regarded. So did they in many general councils, which purposely I will not recite; for all wise men know that acts of parliament are not for God's law in respect of God's law, but in respect of the people.

Now what we are, God knoweth, and all the world seeth; more meet a great deal to have the devil's decrees, than God's religion; so great is our contempt in it. And there-fore justly for our sins, as Job saith, God hath set hypocrites to reign over us; which can no more abide God's true religion, than the owl the light, or bleared eyes the bright sun. For it will have them to do their duties, and walk in diligent doing of the works of their vocation. If God's word, I mean, had place, bishops could not play chancellors and idle prelates, as they do; priests should be otherwise known than by their shaven crowns and appetites. But enough of this. I will now return to the third commodity coming by the cross.

<small>Job xxxiv.</small>

Here let us see the wisdom of God, in making the wisdom of the world foolish. For it knoweth little of man's corruption, how foul it is in the sight of God, and displeaseth him. It knoweth little the portion of God's people to be in another world. It knoweth little the portion of Christians, Christ Jesus. It knoweth little the judgments of God, the great malice of Satan to God's people, the price and estimation of the gospel. And therefore in the cross it seeth not, as God's wisdom would men should see, namely, that God in punishing them which sin least, would have his anger against sin better considered and feared; and that in punishing his people here, he kindleth their desire towards their restful and peaceable home. For in punishing his servants in this life, he doth by these means conform and make them like to Christ; that as they be like in suffering, so they may be partakers in reigning. In punishing his church in the world, he doth thereby give even a demonstration of his judgment, which shall come on all men, when the godly shall there find rest, though now they be afflicted; and the wicked now wallowing in wealth shall be wrapped in woe and smart. In punishing the professors of his gospel on earth, he doth by the same set forth the malice of Satan against the gospel and his people, for the more confirming

<small>The ignorance of worldly wisdom.</small>

<small>Luke xiii.</small>

<small>2 Cor. v.</small>

<small>Philipp. i.</small>

<small>2 Thess. i.
2 Pet. ii.</small>

<small>Job i.
Acts xvi.
xvii. xviii.
&c.</small>

of their faith, and the gospel to be God's word indeed, and them to be God's people: for else the devil would let them alone. In punishing the lovers of his truth more than others which care not for it, he thereby putteth them in mind, how they have not had in price, as they should have had, the rule of his word and gospel. Before such trial and experience by trouble, perchance they thought they had believed and had had faith; which now they see was but a lip faith, a mock faith, or an opinion. All which things we see are occasions for us to take better heed by means of the cross. Psalm cxix.

Therefore, thirdly, let us see the cross to be commodious for us to learn God's wisdom, and what is man's foolishness, God's displeasure at sin, how the elect desire to be with God, and their conformity with Christ, the general judgment, the malice of Satan, hatred of sin, the gospel to be God's word, and how it is much to be esteemed, &c. Thus much for this.

Now will I briefly shew you the cross to be profitable for us, to learn and behold better the providence, presence, and power of God; that all these may be coupled together, as in a chain, to hang about our necks: I mean God's justice, mercy, wisdom, power, presence, and providence. The fourth commodity of the cross.

When all things be in rest, and men be not in trouble, then are they forgetful of God commonly, and attribute too much to their own wisdoms, policies, provisions and diligence; as though they were the procurers of their own fortune and the workers of their own wealth. But when the cross cometh, and that in such sort as their wits, policies, and friends cannot help them, then though the wicked despair and run from God to their anodynes, saints, and unlawful means, yet do the godly therein behold the presence, providence, and power of God. For the scripture teacheth, that all things, weal and woe, should be considered as God's work, although Satan, the devil, be the instrument by whom God worketh justly and mercifully; justly to the wicked, and mercifully to the godly; as by the ensamples of wicked Saul and godly Job we may easily see God's work by Satan his instrument in them both. Amos iii. Isai. xlv. Matth. x.
The devil is God's instrument.

The children of God, therefore, which before forgat God in prosperity, are now in adversity awaked to see God and his work; and no more to hang on their own forecasts, power, friends, wisdom, riches, &c.; but learn to commit themselves unto God's providence and power, whereby they are so preserved and governed, and very often even miraculously delivered, that the very wicked cannot but see God's providence, presence, and power in the cross and affliction of his children; as these (his children, I mean) to their joy do feel it, thereby learning to know God to be the governor of all things. He it is that giveth peace, he it is that sendeth war, he giveth plenty and poverty, he setteth up and casteth down, he bringeth to death, and after giveth life; his presence is everywhere, his providence is within and without, his power is the pillar whereby the godly stand, and to it they lean, as to a thing no less able to set up than to cast down.

<small>Isai. xlv.
Hos. ii.
1 Kings ii.
Luke i.
Psalm cxxxix.</small>

<small>2 Pet. iii.</small>

Which thing full well the apostle saw in his afflictions, and therefore rejoiced greatly in them, that *eminentia virtutis Dei*, God's power might singularly be seen therein.

<small>2 Cor. i.</small>

Concerning this I might bring forth innumerable ensamples of the affliction of God's children, both in the old and new Testament, wherein we may see how they felt God's presence, providence, and power plentifully. But I will omit ensamples; because every one of us that have been or be in trouble, cannot but by the same the rather remember God's presence, which we feel by his hand upon us presently; his providence, which leaveth us not uncared for, without any of our own provision; his power, which both preserveth us from many other evils, that else would come upon us, and also maketh us able to bear more than we thought we could have done. So very often doth he deliver us by such means as have been thought most foolish, and little to be regarded.

<small>Presence.
Providence.
Power.</small>

And, therefore, we spake of our sleep of security and forgetting of God, our trust and shift in our own policy, our hanging on men and on our own power. So that the cross, you see, is commodious, fourthly, for us, to see God's presence, providence, and power; and our own negligence, forgetfulness of God, security, love, trust, and confidence in ourselves and in things of this life to be cut off, as the others are to be taken hold upon.

And this shall suffice for the commodities that come by the cross; wherethrough we may be in love for it for the commodities' sake, which at length we shall find, though presently in sense we feel them not. "No castigation or punishment is sweet or joyous for the present time, but grievous; nevertheless afterward it bringeth the quiet fruit of righteousness unto them which are exercised therein." As we see in medicines, the more wholesome they be, the more unpleasant oftentimes is the taste, as in purgations, pills, and such like bitter things; yet upon the physician's word we will gladly drink them for the profit which cometh of them. And, dearly beloved, although to lose life, goods, or friends for God's gospel's sake seem a bitter and sour thing; yet seeing our Physician which cannot lie, Jesus Christ, I mean, telleth me, that it is very wholesome, howsoever it be toothsome[1], let us with good cheer take the cup at his hand, and drink it merrily. If the cup seem unpleasant, and the drink is bitter, let us put some sugar therein, even a piece of that which Moses cast into the bitter water, and made it pleasant; I mean an ounce or quantity of Christ's afflictions and cross, which he suffered for us. *Heb. xii.* *Exod. xv.* *1 Pet. iv.*

If we call these to mind, and cast of them into our cup, considering what he was, what he suffered, of whom, for whom, to what end, and what came thereof; surely we cannot loathe our medicine, but mix and drink it lustily. Lustily, therefore, drink the cup; Christ giveth it, and will give it unto you, my good brethren and sisters: I mean, prepare yourselves to suffer whatsoever God may lay upon you for the confession of his holy name; if not because of these three things, that you be not of this world, that ye suffer not alone, and your trouble shall not hurt you; yet because of the commodities that come of the cross, I beseech you heartily to embrace it.

[1 Probably a mistake for *untoothsome*.]

CHAPTER V.

HOW THE PAPISTS HOLD THEIR FOUR SPECIAL ARTICLES, THAT THEY CHIEFLY PERSECUTE FOR.

AND here, because the persecution and cross which is come and will come upon us, is specially for these four points of religion, namely, of the sacrament of Christ's body and blood, and for the sacrifice of Christ, for praying for the dead, and for praying to the dead, that is, to saints; I am purposed by God's grace to write hereof a little unto you, thereby to confirm you in the truth, to your comfort in the cross about the same. And first, concerning the first doctrine, what they would have us believe on these points.

Of the Sacrament.

John vi.

This is their doctrine. The catholic church hath taught, as she hath learned and received of Christ, how that he in his last supper, according to his promise, when he promised to give a bread, even his flesh, in instituting the sacrament of the altar (as they call it) performed the same, and that as in all things which he promised he was found true, so in this the catholic church hath believed and doth believe no less. And therefore so soon as the priest in the mass hath fully spoken these words, "This is my body," if he purpose or his intention be as he speaketh, (for that is requisite, teach they,) then that which before was bread, and seemeth to the eye to be bread, is made in very deed Christ's body, flesh, blood, and bone, even the selfsame which was crucified, rose again, and ascended up into heaven. So that he which believeth not this, is a most heinous heretic, and cut off from the catholic church, and is not meet to receive this holy sacrament; because he cannot without this faith of Christ's natural, real, corporal, and carnal body, under the form or accident of bread and wine, otherwise receive this sacrament than unworthily and to eternal damnation. This is a short sum of their doctrine concerning the supper.

Now concerning the sacrifice they teach, that though our Saviour himself did indeed make a full and perfect sacrifice, propitiation, and satisfaction for the sins of all the whole world, never more so, that is to say, bloodily, to be offered again; yet in the supper he offered the same sacrifice to his Father, but unbloodily, that is to say, in will and desire; which is accounted often even for the deed, as this was. Which unbloody sacrifice he commanded his church to offer in remembrance of his bloody sacrifice, as the principal mean whereby his bloody sacrifice is applied both to the quick and dead; as baptism is the mean by the which regeneration is applied by the priest to the infant or child that is baptized. For in that the supper of Christ is to them not only a sacrament, but also a sacrifice, and that not only applicatory, but also propitiatory, because it applieth the propitiatory sacrifice of Christ to whom the priest or minister will, be he dead or alive; and in that, even from the beginning, the fathers were accustomed in the celebration of the supper to have a memorial of the dead[1]; and also in that this sacrifice is a sacrifice of the whole church; the dead being members of the church, of charity, as they cannot but offer for them, even so they cannot but pray for them after the ensample of the catholic church; because it is a wholesome thing, saith Judas Maccabeus, to pray for the dead, that they may be delivered from their sins. Whereunto all the doctors do consent, say they. *Prayer for the dead.* [2 Mac. xii. 44, 45.]

Now, as for praying to saints, they teach, that albeit there is but one Mediator of redemption, yet of intercession the holy saints of God departed this life may well be counted mediators. And, therefore, it is a point of a lowly heart and humble spirit, which God well liketh, to call upon the saints to pray for us first, lest by our presumption to come into God's presence, we being so unworthy, and God being so excellent and full of majesty, we more anger and displease God; whereas by their help God may be entreated to make us more worthy to come unto him, and the sooner to grant us our petitions. For if the holy saints of God, here being upon the earth, could and would pray for the people, obtaining many things at God's hand; it is much more to be believed now, say they, that they can and will, if we pray to them, obtain for us our humble and godly desires. And therefore to the end their sacrifice propitiatory, which in the *Prayer to saints.*

[1 On this subject see Bingham's *Origines Ecclesiasticæ*, Lib. xv. chap. iii. sect. 15—17.]

mass they offer, may be the more available, they use about it much praying to saints. So of these four, as of four pillars, the mass standeth. The which mass, you may see what it is, and how precious and worthy a piece of work it is, by their doctrine concerning the supper, the sacrifice, the praying for the dead and to the dead; whereof I have given you a sum in the most honest, godly, and religious wise, that the best of them do set it forth in. For else, if I should have shewed you this their doctrine, as some of them set it forth, as I know you would abhor it, so the subtle papists would say that I railed and misrepresented them. Therefore because they shall have no such occasion, nor you by their most subtle colours be deceived, I have, in the best manner I can, repeated a sum of their doctrine. The which to the end you might the better consider and have, I will now tell you, as God's word teacheth, how these four points are to be believed and received; and then will I open the filthiness and abomination, which in this their doctrine is devilishly contained.

CHAPTER VI.

HOW GOD'S WORD TEACHETH OF THE SUPPER, WITH CONFUTATION OF THE PAPISTS' HERESY OF TRANSUBSTANTIATION ABOUT THE SAME.

CONCERNING the supper of our Lord, which Christ Jesus did institute to be a sacrament of his body and blood, we believe that his words in the same supper accordingly are to be understood, that is, sacramentally, as he meant them; and not simply, contrary to his meaning, as the papists wrest them. And this is taught us, not only by innumerable such like places, as where baptism is called regeneration, because it is a sacrament of it; circumcision is called God's covenant, because it is a sacrament of it; but also by the plain circumstances of the text, as thereof the evangelists with the apostle St Paul do write plainly, affirming that our Saviour Christ did give, and his disciples did eat, that which he took and

<small>Titus iii.
Gen. xvii.
Matth. xxvi.
Mark xiv.
Luke xxii.
1 Cor. x. xi.</small>

brake, and bade them divide among themselves, that is, bread and wine. For we may not think that Christ's natural body was broken, nor that his blood can be divided. And plainly, our Saviour saith concerning the cup, that he would not drink any more of the fruit of the vine, (which is not his blood, I trow, but wine,) until he should drink it new with them after his resurrection. Matth. xxvi.
Mark xiv.

But to make this matter more plain, like as many things in Christ's supper were figuratively done and spoken, as the washing of the disciples' feet, the paschal lamb was called the passah, Judas was said to have lifted up his heel against him; so doth Luke and Paul plainly alter the words concerning the cup, calling that the new Testament, which Matthew and Mark call his blood; yea, expressly five times the apostle calleth the sacrament of Christ's body after the consecration spoken (as they term it) bread. "Is not the bread, which we break," saith he, "the communion of Christ's body?" Whose exposition I will more boldly stick unto, than unto all the papists' dreams, as long as I sleep not with them, by God's grace. They have none other sentence but these four words, "This is my body." But ask them, what this is, and they will not say, as the apostle doth, namely, that it is bread. No; then they will say, that we hang all by reason, the matter being a matter of faith. Whereas they themselves altogether hang on reason, as though Christ cannot be able to do that which he promiseth, (bread still in substance remaining, as the accidents do,) except it be transubstantiate. Is not this, trow you, to make it a matter of reason, and to hedge God's power in within the limits of reason? If Christ's words that follow, "which is given for you," be to be understood for, "which shall be given, or shall be betrayed for you," and not so precisely, as they be spoken, (for that were to make Christ a liar;) why is it so heinous a matter with the papists, because we do not so precisely take the words immediately going before, namely, "This is my body," as to admit, that if there be bread, then Christ is a liar? Might not we reason and say, Then if Christ's body at the time was not betrayed, (as indeed it was not,) nor his blood shed, then is Christ a liar. But here they will say, All men may know that Christ by the present tense meant the future tense; and in the scripture it is a most usual thing so to take tense for tense. And, I pray you, why may not we say, that all men may know it is most common in scripture to give unto signs the names of the things which they signify? And no man is so foolish, but he knoweth that Christ then instituted a sacrament, wholly sacramentally to be understood; that is, that the sign or visible sacrament should have not only the name of the thing signified, but also some similitude therewith, or else it were no sacrament. But take bread away, as the papists do, leaving there but the accidents only, which do not feed the body; and then what shall resemble and represent unto us Christ's body broken for the food of the soul? As wine comforteth the heart, so doth Christ's blood shed on the cross comfort the soul. But take wine away by transubstantiation, as the papists do, and tell me, what similitude remaineth? None at all: so no sacrament at all. So Christ's institution is taken away. Well do they reject God's commandment for their tradition's sake.

Our faith, therefore, is, that the supper of the Lord is the sacrament of Christ's body and blood. These words, "This is my body, which is broken for you; this is my blood of the new Testament, which is shed for your sins," are most true words, and plain according to Christ's meaning to all them which do as he biddeth them, that is, to all such as take, eat, and drink. Which words the papists keep in their purse, or else their private masses could not stand. To such, I say, as take and eat this sacrament, in sorrowing for their sinful life past, and purposing to amend, above all things remembering and believing that Christ's body was broken for their sins, and his blood shed for their iniquities; all such, I say, as verily as they see, take, taste, and eat bread, and drink wine, which goeth into their body, feedeth it, and nourisheth it; even so verily the soul and spirit by faith receiveth, not only Christ's body broken, or his blood shed, (for "the flesh profiteth nothing, it is the spirit that quickeneth," saith Christ;) but even whole Christ, into whom they are incorporate and made one with him, flesh of his flesh, and bone of his bones. That is to say, as Christ's body is immortal and glorious, even so are theirs now by faith and hope, and at the [last] day they shall be in very deed. Than which thing what can be greater? This we teach and believe concerning this sacrament, detesting and

John vi.

Ephes. v.

abhorring the horrible error of transubstantiation, which maketh bread and wine our God and Christ; and causeth men to be gazers, gapers, and worshippers, yea, idolaters, rather than tasters and eaters, as Christ commandeth; and which maketh Christ's sacrifice of none effect, as now shall be shewed by God's grace.

For this shall suffice to the declaration of our faith concerning the Lord's supper; whereunto agreeth the catholic church, and all the fathers; as full well thou mayest see in the bishop of Canterbury's book, which is far from being answered either by the bishop of Winchester his book in English, or Marcus Constantius in Latin[1], which thou needest no more to confirm thy faith in this matter, than to read them with an indifferent mind, not being addict otherwise than to the desire of the truth. As for this doctrine of transubstantiation, it is a new-found thing about six hundred years old; even then brought out, when Satan was let loose after a thousand years that was bound. Even then was it established, when there was more mischief among the prelates, specially the popes, about the see of Rome, who could catch it, than ever there was among the emperors for the empire. In the primitive church popes were martyred for Christ's spouse's sake, that is, the church; but now one poisoned another, and one slew another, for the rose-coloured whore of Babylon's sake, that is, the popish church. In one hundred and sixty years there was near hard fifty popes[2]; whereas in no such time there were above thirty-three emperors. And in the midst of this miserable state and time this doctrine of transubstantiation was the pope's beginning, as they might have leisure from conspiring against princes, and one against another, to establish it as the very principal pillar of all their power. And no marvel: for this being admitted, then have they power over Christ the King of all kings, that he be where they will, when they will, and as long as they will, under their power; wherethrough the

_{Rev. xx.}

_{Rev. xvii. xviii.}

[1 By Marcus Constantius is meant bishop Gardiner, who under this fictitious name published his *Confutatio cavillationum, &c*. See archbishop Cranmer's writings and disputations relative to the Lord's supper. Parker Soc. Ed. p. 419. note.]

[2 The period alluded to is probably contained between the beginning of the tenth and the latter part of the eleventh century.]

other must needs follow, that if they have power over Christ, and that in heaven, to bring him down at their pleasure, much more then over all earth, emperors, kings, princes, and people; yea, even over the devil, purgatory, and hell, have they full power and jurisdiction, being now gods on earth, which sit in the holy place, even as God, yea, above God; to make what article of faith shall please them, as they have done this of transubstantiation; which might as well be denied as granted, saith Duns, one of their own doctors, and master Gabriel also, if it so pleased the holy father, and his spouse the church of Rome[1]. Before this time all the fathers' diligence, labour, and care was to call men to the receiving of this sacrament for the confirmation of their faith; that as verily as they did eat bread and drink wine here, so should they not doubt but that by faith they did feed on the body of Christ, broken for their sins, and on his blood shed for their iniquities. And therefore sometimes would they call the sacrament bread, a figure or a sign; sometime would they call it the body and blood of our Saviour Jesus Christ, as the nature of sacraments is to be called with the name of the things which they do signify; that thereby men's minds might be withdrawn from the consideration of sensible and visible things to things heavenly, which they do signify and represent. And their care and crying unto the people was to receive it; and therefore they made decrees that such as would not receive and be present, should be spurned out of the church. Oh, how earnest was Chrysostom herein! Read his sixty-first homily unto the people of Antioch[2]. But after that this decree and doctrine of transubstantiation came in, no crying out hath there been to receive it, (no, that is the prerogative of the priest and

2 Thess. ii.

Scotus super 4. Senten. dist. 11. Gabriel. super canon. missæ. Lect. 40.

[1 Joann. Duns Scoti Opera, Lugd. 1639, in Lib. IV. Sentent. Dist. XI. Quæst. 3. Tom. VIII. pp. 6, 16, 18, 19; and Gabriel Biel. Canon. Miss. Expos. Basil. 1515. Lect. XL. fol. 94, 2. The passages are referred to by archbishop Cranmer in his second book against Transubstantiation, p. 302, Parker Society's Edition; and they are given at length in his *Defensio veræ et Catholicæ doctrinæ de Sacramento corporis et sanguinis Christi Servatoris nostri*, p. 34. Ib.]

[2 The homily referred to is the 61st ad Pop. Antioch. in the Latin edition of Chrysostom, and will be found Tom. V. p. 336. ed. Paris. 1570.]

shaven shorelings;) but altogether the end of their crying out was as now to believe transubstantiation, Christ to be their flesh, blood, and bone at every altar, between every priest's hands, yea, in every priest's mouth, when it pleaseth them......The crying and teaching of the clergy continually hath been to believe transubstantiation, and then to come to church to see their Maker once a day, to hold up their hands, to knock on their breasts, to streak their faces, to mutter with their Latin prayers, to take holy water and holy bread, to live in obedience to holy father, and holy church his spouse. This was all they required. Drink, dice, card, fight, swear, steal, no matter; so that in the morning they see their God, all is well; good catholic people; no man shall hurt them, or persecute them. But if any man should not allow nor worship this God of their making, although he lived a most godly life, and were a man full of charity, sobriety, and very religious, O, such is an heretic or schismatic. Nothing would please these wolves but even the blood and life of such a poor sheep; as men have felt before, and now begin to feel. Let all the pack of them burthen those justly, whom now they imprison and cause to fly the realm, of any other thing than only of this, that we will not serve their God of bread and wine, and then will we suffer shame. But I have been too long herein. Now to our doctrine and belief, for the second point concerning Christ's sacrifice.

CHAPTER VII.

HOW GOD'S WORD TEACHETH OF CHRIST'S SACRIFICE, AND THE POPE'S BLASPHEMY THEREIN REVEALED.

THE doctrine and faith in this behalf is as in the other, that is, according to God's holy word; namely, that Jesus Christ, the Son of God and second Adam, by whom we receive righteousness unto life, as by the first Adam we received sin unto death,—our faith is, I say, that this Christ in our flesh, which he took of the substance of the virgin Mary, but pure and without sin, for the satisfying of God's just displeasure deservedly and in our flesh, did in the same suffer unjustly all kinds of misery and affliction, and offered up himself unto his eternal Father with a most willing obedient heart and ready mind, when he was crucified upon the cross. And thereby as he satisfied God's justice, so he merited and procured his mercy, peace, and favour for all them which either before that time were dead, either were at that time present, either that should afterwards come and believe, by and in that offering done for them and their sins; so that God the eternal Father, I say, would be, in this their Christ, their God and Father, and not lay their sins committed to their charge to condemnation.

This doctrine the holy scripture teacheth almost every where; but specially in the Epistle to the Hebrews, chaps. i. vii. viii. ix. This is most lively for faith, how that by one oblation once offered by this Christ himself all that be God's people are sanctified. For as in respect of them that died in God's covenant and election before Christ suffered his death, and offered his sacrifice, one, alone, and omnisufficient, never more to be offered, he is called the Lamb slain from the beginning of the world, and the one alone Mediator between God and man, whose forthcoming was from the beginning; even so in respect of the virtue and efficacy of this one sacrifice to all God's people continually unto the world's end, the Holy Ghost doth tell us, that thereby he hath made holy such as be children of salvation: and saith not, shall make holy, or doth make holy; lest any man

Rev. xiii.
1 Tim. ii.
Mic. iii. v.

should with the papists indeed reiterate this satisfaction again: although in words they say otherwise, as anon we shall see, if hereunto I shew you the means whereby to apply this sacrifice; which I will do very briefly.

For in the seventeenth of John our Saviour doth very plainly shew this in these words: "For their sakes," saith he, "I sanctify myself, that they also might be sanctified through the truth. I pray not for them alone, but for those also which shall believe on me through their preaching." Here our Saviour applieth his sacrifice in teaching and praying for them. And as he teacheth them as ministers to do the like, that is, to preach and pray for the application of his sacrifice to the church, so doth he teach them and all the church to apply it unto themselves by believing it and by faith. The which thing the apostle St Paul in many places, but more plainly in the second to the Corinthians, the first chapter in the latter end, doth teach. Read it and see. So that, as ye have now Christ's one only sacrifice, which he himself on the cross offered once, as sufficient for all that do believe, and never more to be reiterated; so have you, that for the applying of it to his church the ministers should preach, and pray that their preaching might be effectual in Christ. And as Paul was ready himself to suffer death for the confirmation of the faith of the elect, so should the church and every member of the same, which is of years of discretion, by believing in Christ through the minister's preaching, apply it to themselves. As for infants, I need not in this place to speak of God's election. It is most certain this kind of applying, as it killeth the papistical priests, which hate not the dead worse than true preaching, so doth it cast down all their soul-massing and foolish foundations for such as be dead and past the ministry of God's word. And also it putteth away the opinion of *opus operatum*, and perseverance in impiety, from such as would enjoy the benefits of Christ's death.

CHAPTER VIII.

OF PRAYING FOR THE DEAD, THE TRUE DOCTRINE.

Now as concerning the third, that is, praying for the dead and sacrificing for them, as in the other we confess, teach, and believe according to God's word, so do we in this; namely, that in holy scripture, throughout the canonical books of the old and new Testament, we find neither precept nor ensample of praying for any, when they be departed this life; but as men die, so shall they arise: if in faith in the Lord towards the south, then need they no prayers; then are they presently happy, and shall arise in glory: if in unbelief without the Lord towards the north, then are they past all help, in the damned state presently, and shall rise to eternal shame. Wherefore according to the scripture we exhort men to repent, and while they have time, to work well. Every man shall bear his own burthen; every man shall give account for himself, and not for John, nor for Thomas, that sing and pray for him. Every man shall receive according to that he himself doeth in this body, while he is here alive, be it good or bad; and not according to that his executors, or this chantry priest and that fraternity doth for him. Whereby we may well see, if we will, that as prayer for the dead is not available or profitable to the dead, so is it of us not allowable, or to be excused. For as they that are departed are past our prayers, being either in joy or in misery, as is above shewed; even so we, having for it no word of God, whereupon faith leaneth, cannot but sin in doing it, in that we do it not of faith, because we have no word of God for it. Therefore with Abraham, Isaac, Jacob, Moses, the prophets, Christ Jesus, and the apostles, we bury the dead in a convenient place, and mourn in measure, as men having hope of the resurrection, not because of them, for that were a great point of ingratitude, they being departed out of miserable condition unto a most blessed state. Therefore we give thanks to God for them, praise his name for his power and might shewed in them, and pray that we may depart in the same faith, and joyfully rise with them in

Eccles. xi.

John v.

Gal. v.
Coloss. iii.
Rom. xiv.

2 Cor. v.

Rom. x. xiv.

1 Thess. iv.

Rev. xiv.

the resurrection; which we desire and wish the Lord would hasten. We mourn, I say, not because of them, but of ourselves, that have lost the company of such our helpers, and further us in spiritual and temporal benefits, by them being admonished of our immortality and of the vanity of this life, that we might the more contemn it, and desire the everlasting life, where they and we shall never be separated.

This is our faith and doctrine for them that be departed; who though they be members of the same holy mystical body of Christ that we be of, yet should they in this case be discerned from the militant members, they being at rest, and 2 Tim. iv. having finished their course and fight, in no point needing any of our help, unless we should too arrogantly set up our own merits and prayers, and pull down Christ, as though we were able to get pardon and higher crown in heaven for others; where all our righteousness and the best thing we do is so far from helping others, that thereby we cannot help ourselves; but had need to cry, *Dimitte nobis debita nostra*, being no better in God's sight than a defiled woman's cloth, although to the Luke xi. sight of men they may seem gorgeous and gay. For if the Isai. lxiv. papists would say, (as, when they are pressed with blasphemy in extolling their own merits and works of supererogation against Christ, they use,) that our prayers do them no good in respect of the worthiness of their prayers, but in respect of God's goodness, in that God's goodness is not to be looked for otherwise than he hath promised; let them either give men his promise, or else in this behalf keep silence, and exercise themselves better in doing their duties to their brethren that be alive; towards whom their charity is very cold, although when they are dead, then they will pretend much, then will they pray for them, but yet not for nought and freely, as true charity worketh; for no penny, no paternoster. Give nothing, and then they will neither sing nor say *requiem*, nor *placebo*, I warrant you. But of this sufficient. Now to the last, of praying to the dead, or to saints departed this life.

CHAPTER IX.

OF PRAYING TO SAINTS.

HERE we confess, teach, and believe, as before is said, according to God's holy word, that as all and every good thing cometh only from God the Father by the means of Jesus Christ, so for the obtaining of the same we must call upon his holy name, as he by himself commandeth very often. But forasmuch as God dwelleth in light inaccessible, and is a consuming fire, and hateth all impiety and uncleanness, and we be blind, stubble, grass, hay, and nothing but filth, unclean, and sinful; and because that therefore, as we may not, so we dare not approach to his presence; it hath pleased this good God and Father of his love to send a spokesman and mediator, an intercessor and advocate between him and us, even Jesus Christ, his dearly beloved Son; by whom we might have free entrance with boldness to come before his presence and throne of mercy, to find and obtain grace and help in time of need. For this our Mediator and Advocate is with his Father of the same substance, power, wisdom, and majesty, and therefore may weigh well with him in all things; and with us he is of the same substance which we are of, even flesh and man, but pure and without sin, in all things being tempted like unto us, and having experience of our infirmities; that he might be merciful and faithful in our behalf, to purge us from our sins, and to bring us into such favour with the Father, that we might be not only dearly beloved through him, the only dearling of the Father, but also obtain whatsoever we shall ask, according to his word and will, in the name of this same our Mediator, Saviour, Intercessor, and Advocate. So that easy it is to see, that as it is an obedient service to God the Father, to call always upon him in all our need; so to come to his presence through Christ is to the honour of Christ's mediation, intercession, and advocateship. And therefore, as it cannot be but against the Almighty God and Father, to ask or look for any thing elsewhere, at the hands of any that be departed this life, as though he were not the giver of all good things, or as though he had not commanded us to come unto him; so we

[margin: James i. / Psal. l. / 1 Tim. vi. / Heb. xiii. Psal. v. / Heb. ii. iv. / Heb. iii. iv. / 1 Pet. ii. / Matt. iii. xvii. / Matt. vii. / 1 John v. / John xiv. / Psal. l.]

see it is manifestly against Christ Jesus our Lord, by any other saint, angel, or archangel, to come and move any thing at our Father's hands, as though he were not our Mediator, Advocate, and Intercessor, or else not a sufficient Mediator, Advocate, or Intercessor, or at least not so merciful, meek, gracious, loving, and ready to help, as others: whereas he only so loved us, as the very hearts of all men and angels never were able to conceive any part of the height, depth, breadth, and length of the same, as it is. If his own heart-blood was not too dear for us, being his very enemies, and never desirous to do his will; how is it possible that he will contemn us for coming unto him with purpose and desire to serve him? Ephes. iii.

Many other reasons I could give you, wherefore the saints are not to be prayed unto; for that pulleth from faith in Christ: it maketh them gods; it is idolatry, &c. But this may suffice. So that now you see by God's word, what our faith is concerning these four things. Which that you may the more love, embrace, and be content to carry with you through fire and water, I will now go about with God's grace, as briefly as I can, to shew how abominable their doctrine is, even out of the short sum thereof already before by me rehearsed.

CHAPTER X.

THE POPISH DOCTRINE OF THE SACRAMENT CONFUTED MORE LARGELY.

FIRST, where they allege the catholic church to have taught concerning the supper the doctrine of transubstantiation, of Christ's real and carnal presence, dearly beloved, know that this is a manifest lie. For as the catholic church never knew of it for nine hundred years at the least after Christ's ascension; so after that time no other church did obstinately defend, cruelly maintain, and wilfully wrest the scriptures and doctors for the establishing of it, save only the popish church, and their own doctors, Duns and Gabriel, do teach[1]. Transubstantiation is a new doctrine.

[1 See above, p. 254.]

Read the bishop of Canterbury's book against Winchester[1], and see. Whereas they say, that Christ in his supper by taking bread and speaking the words of consecration did make it his flesh, according to his promise in John, when he saith, "And the bread which I will give is my flesh, &c.;" so that they would thereby seem to have two places of scripture for this their doctrine of transubstantiation and real or carnal presence; although diversly I could improve[2] this, yet because for that I would not be over tedious unto you, even by the same their sentence you shall see how learnedly they lie.

John vi. appears as marginal note.

The sentence is this: "And the bread that I will give is my flesh, which I will give for the life of the world." First mark that he saith, "The bread is my flesh." He saith not, "shall be my flesh," but it "is my flesh." This, I trow, maketh against them; for the sacrament a year after at the least was not instituted. Again he saith, that the bread is his flesh, which he will give for the life of the world. Here would I ask them, whether Christ's death was for the life of the world, or in vain. If they say it was for the life of the world, then why do they apply and give it to the sacrament? Was it crucified? Or if it be the same sacrifice, (for so they say,) either it was effectual, or not. If it was effectual, then Christ's death needed not. If it was not effectual, then Christ was not God, and could not do that he would. Thus ye may see their ungodly foolishness, or foolish ungodliness, I cannot tell which to call it well. Whereas they require the intent of the priest to consecrate Christ's body; forasmuch as we know not any man's intent, (God only knoweth the heart,) yea, the words we know not, they are so spoke in *hucker mucker;* I pray you, in what a doubtfulness are we brought whether it be the sacrament or not! In what peril are we of worshipping a piece of bread for our Christ! Is not this, trow you, sweet and comfortable gear, that a man shall always stand in doubt whether he have received the sacrament or not? Whereas they will have it bread to the eye, and not to the mouth, judge then, whether a dog may not eat Christ's body; judge whether the devil, if he would come in the likeness of a priest, might not swallow up

[1] Archbishop Cranmer's *Answer to a Crafty and Sophistical Cavillation devised by Stephen Gardiner.*]

[2] Improve: disprove.]

Christ, and so bring him into hell, from whence, because there is no redemption there, Christ's body should never come, but be damned. Judge, whether the taste of thy mouth is not as much to be credited, as the sight of the eye; specially in that the scripture so often calleth it bread after the consecration, as before I have shewed. Judge, whether Christ's body be not very petty, that it can be in so little a room. Judge, whether Christ hath more bodies than one, when perchance the priest hath twenty or a hundred before him. Judge, whether the priest brake not Christ's body in breaking of it. Judge, whether it be seemly to chew Christ's body with the teeth. Judge, whether Christ did eat his own body; yea, or no? Christ did eat the sacrament with his disciples. Judge, whether it be seemly that Christ should be kept so in prison, as they keep him. Judge, whether it be seemly that Christ's body should be so dindle-dandled and used, as they use it. Judge, whether the people, knocking and kneeling at the elevation of that they see, (for they see but the forms of bread and wine, and not Christ's body, if it be as the papists feign;) judge, I say, whether the people by the papists' own doctrine be not made idolaters.

Many more absurdities there be, which I purposely omit. This little is enough hereby to give you occasion to know the more. Where they say that the bread is made Christ's body, flesh, blood, &c., that is, that Christ's body is made of the bread; as the bishop of Winchester in his book for this matter of the *Devil's Sophistry* and elsewhere doth affirm; you may see how shamelessly, yea, blasphemously they speak. For Christ's body crucified was born of the virgin Mary, even of her substance; but they say the supper is that body which was crucified. Now, I trow, bread is one thing, and the virgin's flesh another thing: therefore indeed they deny Christ in the flesh, that they may stablish their Christ in the bread; which is the very root of antichrist. Last of all, whereas they say that they receive the sacrament to damnation, which do not believe their transubstantiation; if with Paul their words were conferred, you should see otherwise. For he saith, they receive this bread (for so he calleth it after the words of consecration) unworthily, which do not esteem

Christ's body: as indeed the papists do not, which would bring Christ down out of heaven for thieves and whores to chew and eat, for moths to corrupt, and to be in danger of moulding; as, if they kept their hosts long, indeed they will mould, and then will they burn them. Do these men, trow you, esteem Christ's body? Paul plainly sheweth in the same place, that the wicked man which receiveth the sacrament unworthily, eateth not Christ's body, but his own damnation, which I trow be not Christ's body. And this shall serve for this time to shew you, how shameless, filthy, and abominable this their doctrine of transubstantiation is. If in so short a sum of their doctrine there be so many abominations, I pray you, how much is in the whole sum of the same? Now for the sacrifice.

CHAPTER XI.

THE POPISH DOCTRINE OF THE SACRIFICE CONFUTED.

FIRST, in that they grant Christ's sacrifice on the cross done by himself to be full and perfect enough, we may well see that we need not this which they have found out, indeed to make the other imperfect; for else it needed no reiteration. But seeing they reiterate it by this, and make it needful even as baptism, easily may all men know, that though they speak one thing, they mean another, and so are dissemblers and destroyers of Christ's sacrifice, little considering the great pain that Christ suffered, seeing they weigh it no better.

Whereas they say, that it is the same sacrifice which Christ offered on the cross, but unbloodily, (wherein they seem to deny transubstantiation; for else I trow it must needs be bloody,) I would thus reason with them. Inasmuch as Christ's sacrifice on the cross was the only perfect and all-sufficient propitiatory sacrifice for the sins of the world, as they confess; this could not be the same, because it was done before that upon the cross. Or else the full perfect sacrifice was then in the supper finished, and so Christ's death is in vain, and a foolish thing. If Christ's death be not foolish, but indeed, as it is, the full and perfect sacrifice for the sins of the world; then this, which they feign he offered in his last supper, is not the same, prate what pleaseth them; or else it is not of value, take whether they will. Whereas they prate of Christ's will, that it was accepted before his Father for the deed; as they shall never be able to shew one word to prove that Christ would in his supper sacrifice himself to his Father for the sins of the world, (for there is not one word thereof throughout the whole bible,) so do they belie God the Father, which would indeed have his Son to drink the cup that he prayed to be taken from him, or else make Christ's death frustrate and more than need; which is the only thing that all their doctrine tendeth unto. For if the Father alloweth his will for the deed, I pray you, who seeth not now the deed to be more than is needed?

Where they say, that Christ commanded his church to offer this sacrifice to his Father in remembrance of his bloody sacrifice; I would pray them to shew me, where he commanded it, and then good enough. But, dearly beloved, they can never shew it. If they will say, *hoc facite*, to take *facere* for *to sacrifice*, as some teach it; then will I say, that a boy of twelve years old can tell they lie. For *hoc facite, do you this*, pertaineth to the whole action of Christ's supper, of taking, eating, and drinking of the sacrament, &c., and as well spoken to the laymen as the priests: but I trow they will not suffer the laymen to say mass another while for them. No, this were too much against their honour, and gain also.

But if one would ask them, what they offer to the Father, then a man should see their abominations. For if they should say nothing, then men would take them as they be, liars. If they say, bread and wine, as indeed they do in their mass horribly; then in that they say they offer the same thing which Christ offered on the cross, and he offered his body, bread must needs be Christ's body, and so Christ's body is bread and wine. If they say, that they offer up Christ, in that the offerer must needs be as good at the least, yea, a better than the thing offered, then must they needs shew themselves open antichrists. For they make themselves equal with Christ, yea, better than he: which thing indeed their holy father and grandsire the pope doth. For where Christ would take upon him to teach nothing, but what he had received of his Father, and therefore willed men to search the scriptures, as all his apostles did, whether their doctrine was not according thereunto; the pope and his prelates will be bold to teach what please them more than God biddeth, yea, clean contrary to that which God biddeth; as it is plain by all these four points, transubstantiation, sacrifice, praying for the dead, and to the dead. But see, I pray you, these abominations. The sacrifice of Christ for the redemption of the world was not simply his body and his blood, but his body broken and his blood shed, that is, all his passion and suffering in his body and flesh. In that therefore they offer, as they say, the same sacrifice which Christ offered, dearly beloved, do they not, as much as in them is, kill, slay, whip, and crucify Christ again with wretches and antichrists? Who would not desire to die for his master Christ's cause against this their heinous and stinking abomination?

Whereas they call this sacrifice of the mass the principal mean to apply the benefit of Christ's death to the quick and dead, I would gladly have them to shew, where and of whom they learned it. Sure I am they learned it not of Christ. For when he sent his disciples abroad to apply unto men the benefit of his death, he bade them not mass it, but preach the gospel, as the mean by the which God had appointed believers to be saved. The which thing Peter told Cornelius plainly; as Paul also teacheth almost every where in his epistles. But indeed preaching they may not away with, as well for that it is too painful, as for that it is nothing so gainful, nor of authority and estimation in the world. Nothing so displeaseth the devil as preaching the gospel, as in all ages easily we may well see, if we will mark to our comfort in this age. And therefore by giving his daughter idolatry, with her dowry of worldly wealth, riches, and honour, to the pope and his shaven shorelings, they have by this means in many years been begetting a daughter, which at length was delivered to destroy preaching, even the minion *Missa;* mistress Missa, who danced daintily before the Herods of the world, and is the cause even why John the Baptist and the preachers be put into prison and lose their heads. This dancing damsel, the darling of her mother, the fair garland of her fathers (for she hath many fathers), the gaudy gallant of her grandsire, is trimmed and tricked in the best and most holy manner or wise that can be, even with the word of God,

Matt. xxviii.
Mark xvi.
Luke xxiv.

Acts x.

Col. i. ii.
2 Cor. v.

the epistle and the gospel, with the sacrament of Christ's body and blood, with the pomander[1] and perfumes of prayer, and all goodly things that can be; but blasphemously and horribly abused to be a mermaid to amuse and bewitch men, sailing in the seas of this life to be enamoured on her. And therefore besides her aforesaid goodly apparel, she hath all kinds of sweet tunes, ditties, melodies, singing, playing, ringing, knocking, kneeling, standing, lifting, crossing, blessing, blowing, mouthing, incensing, &c. Moreover she wanteth no gold, silver, precious stones, jewels, and costly silks, velvets, satins, dumasties, &c., and all kind of things which are gorgeous in the sight of men; as, if you call to mind the chalices, copes, vestments, crucifixes, &c., you cannot but see. And hereto is she beautified yet more, to be shewed and set forth in lying words and titles given to her; that she hath all power in heaven, earth, and hell, that she hath all things for soul and body, for quick and dead, for man and beast. And lest men should think her too coy a dame, lo, sir, she offereth herself most gently to all that will come, be they never so poor and stinking and foul, to have their pleasure on her. Come who will, she is "Hail, good fellow;" and that not only to make herself common to them that will, but also to ply them plentifully with most pleasant promises falsely, and giving most licentious liberties to all her lovers, and great fees and wages to her diligent servants and ministers; so that there needeth no preaching of the gospel. She hath all things, she will give all things; the death of Christ she will apply and can to whom she will, and when she will. For this daughter the mothers, the fathers, and the grandfathers watch night and day, as the only mean whereby Herod and Herodias may live as they lust.......But, dearly beloved, as from the devil's dearling indeed, fly from her; and know that the true and only way to apply the benefit of Christ's death and sacrifice, is in the minister's behalf by preaching, and in your behalf by believing.

This is a sacrament, and not a sacrifice; for in this, using it as we should, we receive of God obsignation and full certificate of Christ's body broken for our sins, and his blood shed for our iniquities. As in baptism we are confirmed, and settle ourselves in possession of the promise of salvation to

[1 Pomander: a ball made up of several perfumes.]

appertain unto us, God to be our God, Christ to be our Christ, and we to be God's people; the promise of the word of God giveth and offereth, faith in us applieth and receiveth the same, and the sacraments do confirm and (as it were) seal up: baptism, that we are regenerated with the Spirit of God, made his children, brethren to Christ, and engrafted into him; the supper, that we are fed with Christ spiritually, with his body and blood, yea, that we be incorporated into Christ, to be flesh of his flesh and bone of his bones, as he by being born of the virgin Mary was flesh of our flesh and bone of our bones. Away therefore with their abominable doctrine, that the sacrifice of the mass is the principal means to apply Christ's death to the quick and dead; wherein all men may see that they lie boldly. For as the word of God in the ministry pertaineth not to the dead, (for who will be so mad as to go and preach on dead men's graves, that the dead men may hear?) so likewise do not the sacraments. Little beholden were men to Christ and to the apostles, if this were the principal mean to apply salvation, that they would use it so little, and preach so much. Paul, having respect to the chiefest end wherefore he was sent, said, that he was not sent to baptize, but to preach. And often saith he, that he was an apostle segregate of God to preach the gospel. And the bishop Timothy did he warn to preach in season and out of season, speaking never a word of this massing or sacrificing Christ's body.

1 Cor. i.

Rom. i.
Gal. i.

2 Tim. iv.

Last of all, where they make a similitude, that as by baptism the minister applieth to the child regeneration, so in this, &c. O that this similitude were well looked on! then would it make them to bluster; for they are no more like than an apple like an oyster. In baptism the child is alive, but here the man is dead: in baptism the child is present, but here the man is perchance forty miles off, if he sacrifice for the quick, yea, hundred miles from him: in baptism the child receiveth the sacrament, but here you must look and gape; but beware you take not; for ye may receive but once a year, and then also you must receive but the one half, the cup he will keep from you. In baptism is required God's election, if he be an infant; or faith, if he be of age; and therefore he reciteth the promise, that it may be heard: but here is no faith required; for how can men believe, when they are dead? No promise is then preached or heard. So that even this their similitude maketh the matter plain enough: for baptism all men know to be no sacrifice. But of this I have spoken a little before, that if applying come by the priest's massing, then were preaching in vain, believing in vain, godly life in vain; the priest were God's fellow, yea, Christ's superior, as is aforesaid. Now for the third, of praying for the dead; wherein I will be brief.

CHAPTER XII.

THE CONFUTATION OF THE PAPISTS' SACRIFICING AND PRAYING FOR THE DEAD.

First, when they say, this applicatory sacrifice may be called a propitiatory sacrifice, because it applieth the propitiatory sacrifice to whom the priest will, be he dead or alive; as I would have you to note, how they grant, that of itself it is not a propitiatory sacrifice, whereby they vary from that which they elsewhere teach, that it is the selfsame sacrifice which Christ offered on the cross unbloodily; so, I pray you, forget not, that the priest is God's fellow, for he may apply it to whom he will. Therefore honour sir John, and make much of sir Thomas: for though God could make thee alone, yet alone, without the priest, he cannot save thee. Again, if sir John be thy friend, care neither for God nor the devil; live as thou wilt, he will bring thee to heaven, although thou slip into hell. So they write, that Gregory by massing did with Trajan the emperor. It maketh no matter how thou live here, so thou have the favour of the pope and his shavelings.

Whereas they say, that the fathers from the beginning were accustomed to make memorials for the dead; this I grant to be true, as we do in our communion. But to gather that therefore they prayed for them, it no more followeth, than to say, that our English service doth allow it, where it doth not. For ye must note, that there is a memorial for the dead, as well in giving thanks to God for them, as in praying for them; for to say, to pray for the dead, is a general word, including in it giving of thanks. And therefore when we read in the ancient fathers of the primitive church of memorials for the dead[1], or praying for the dead, it is not to be understood that they prayed for to deliver them from purgatory, (for that was not found out then,) or from hell, (as our papists do in their prayers of the mass,) for there is no redemption; or for pardon of their sins, as though they had it not; for if they depart without it, they are damned; or for to get them a higher place in heaven, for that were injurious to Christ, that we should purchase places and higher crowns in heaven for others: but either for the desire of the more speedy coming of Christ, to hasten the resurrection; either that they might not be thought negligent or careless over the dead; either that the living might be occasioned to increase in love to the church here in earth, who still followeth with good will and love even men when they be departed; either to admonish the church to be diligent over such as live, and careful to extend her love, if it were possible, even to the dead. On this wise should we expound, not only the former, but also the later fathers, as Austin, Chrysostom, and others; which though in some places they seem very manifestly to allow praying for the dead, yet they are not to be understood otherwise than I have said for them. For never knew they of our merits and purgatory; for if they had but dreamed thereon, surely they would have been much more circumspect in their speakings and writings of this, than they were.

Where they say, that because this sacrifice is the sacrifice of the whole church, whereof the dead be members, therefore they should be prayed for; as before I have shewed, that we must put a difference between the members of the church militant here on earth, and those which be now at rest and peace with God; so would I have you to note here, that they should pray for none other dead, than such as be members of Christ's church. Now in that all such die in the Lord, and therefore are happy, I would gladly learn, what good such prayer doeth to those so departed. As for purgatory pike-purse, they pass not upon it. But that this is a sacrifice applicatory or propitiatory, the papists can never prove.

Where they say, charity requireth it; I answer, that inasmuch as charity followeth faith, and will not go a foot

[1 See above, p. 249.]

further than faith sheweth the way; seeing faith is not Rom. x. but of the word of God, and God's word for this they have not, easy it is to perceive that this praying thus for the dead is not of christian charity. But be it that charity required it, I then marvel why they are so uncharitable, that will do nothing herein without money. Why will they not pray without pence? If the pope and his prelates were charitable, they would, I trow, make sweep-stake at once with purgatory.

Where they allege the sentence of the Maccabees; as all men of learning know, the Fathers allow not that book to be God's Spirit or catholic, so do I wonder that in all the old Testament this sacrificing for the dead was never spoken of before. In all the sacrifices that God appointed, we read of never one for the dead.

This gear came not up till the religion was wonderfully corrupt among the Jews: as with us it was never found out till horrible corruption of religion and ignorances of God's word came into the church of God, when preaching was put down, and massing came up. Then faith in Christ was cold, penance became popish, and trust was taught in creatures, ignorance abounded, and look, what the clergy said, that was believed. Then came up visions, miracles, dead spirits walking, and talking how they might be released by this mass, by that pilgrimage gate-going. And so came up this pelf of praying for the dead, which Paul the apostle and all the prophets never spake one word of; for all men may easily see, that it is a thing which helpeth much vice, and hindereth godliness. Who will be so earnest to amend, to make restitution of that he hath gotten unjustly, and live in a godly life, and true fear of God, being taught that by prayers, by masses, by founding of chauntries, &c., when he is gone, he shall find ease and release, yea, and come to joy eternal? Christ's doctrine is, that the way of salvation is strait; but this teaching, heaping of masses one upon another, when we are dead, maketh it wide. Christ's teaching is, that we should live in love and charity, the sun should not go down on our wrath; but this doctrine, to pray for the dead to be delivered out of purgatory, teacheth rather to live in little love, in wrath even to our death's day: for sir John can and will help; sir Thomas, by a mass of *scala cœli* will bring us into heaven. Christ's doctrine is, that he is the way; but this doctrine maketh the massing priest the way: a way indeed it is, but to hell and to the devil. Dearly beloved, therefore take good heart unto you for this gear, rather than you would consent unto it, to lose life and all that ever you have. You shall be sure with Christ to find it, and that for ever, with infinite increase.

Last of all, when they allege the catholic church and consent of all the doctors on this matter; as I wish you should know that to be the true and catholic church which is grounded upon God's word, which word they have not for them in this matter; so would I ye should know that there is no member of the church, but he may err; for they be men, and "all men be liars," as David saith. Now if all the members may err, then you may easily see, whereto your faith ought to lean, even unto God's weighty word. Hear the church and the doctors of the church; but none otherwise, than as teachers, and try their teaching by God's word. If they teach according to it, then believe and obey them; if contrary, then know they be but men, and always let your faith lean to God's word.

Howbeit, for this matter of praying for the dead, know of truth that there be no doctors of four hundred or five hundred years after Christ's ascension, but if they in some places seem to allow praying for the dead, yet they would be taken in some of the senses which I have specified. In many places do they by divers sentences declare it themselves. But of this enough.

CHAPTER XIII.

THE REFUTATION OF THE HERESY OF PRAYING TO SAINTS DEPARTED OUT OF THIS WORLD.

Now to the last, of praying to saints. First, where they say, there be more mediators of intercession than Christ, making a distinction not learned out of God's book, in such sense and for such purpose as they allege; I wish they would look on the epistle to the Romans, and 1 John ii. and there shall they learn to take better heed. The one saith, "Christ [Rom. viii.] sitteth on the right hand of his Father, and prayeth for us:"

the other saith, "He is our advocate," that is, a spokesman, comforter, intercessor, and mediator. Now would I ask them, seeing that Christ is a mediator of intercession, (as I am sure they will grant,) whether he be sufficient or no. If they say, no; then all men will know that they lie. But if they say, yes; then may I ask, why they are not content with sufficient? What fault find ye with him? Is there any more merciful than he, any more desirous to do us good than he? any that knoweth our grief and need so much as he? any that knoweth the way to help us so well as he? No, none so well. He crieth: "Ask, and ye shall have; come to me, _{Matt. vii.} and I will help you; ask, that your joy may be full. Hitherto _{Matt. xi.} ye have not asked any thing in my name." Therefore, my _{John xvi.} good brethren and sisters, let us thank God for this mediator; and as he is our alone mediator for redemption, let us take him even so for intercession. For if by his work of redemption of enemies we are made friends; surely we being friends, and having him above on the right hand of his Father, shall _{Rom. v.} by him obtain all things. _{Heb. i.}

Where they call it a point of a lowly and an humble spirit to go to saints, that they may pray for them; you may easily see, it is a point of an arrogant heart and a false untrue spirit. For inasmuch as God plainly biddeth thee, _{Deut. xii.} that thou put nought to his word, nor take aught therefrom; _{Rev. xxii.} in that his word is, "Thou shalt call upon him in thy need;" _{Psal. l.} why art thou so arrogant and proud, that you will go to Peter or Paul to pray for thee? Where hast thou God's word? Dost thou think God is true of his promise? Why then dost thou not go unto him? Dost thou think that God at any time receiveth thee for thy worthiness? Upon whom be his eyes, but upon him that trembleth at his word? _{Isai. lxv.} Blessed are they that be poor in spirit, and think themselves _{Matt. v.} unworthy of God's help. Wherefore hath God sworn that he wills not the death of a sinner, but that sinners might be _{Ezek. xxxiii.} most certain of his love and mercy to be much greater than they are able to conceive? His mercies are above all his _{Psal. cxlv.} works. But thou, that runnest to saints, thinkest that it is not so; for else wouldest thou go to him thyself, that thou, seeing his so much goodness, mightest the more love him, which thou canst not, if thou use other means than by Christ only.

Where they bring in the ensample of saints praying for the people, and obtaining benefits for them, whilst they were living here on earth, and so gather, that much more they will and can do it now for us, in that they be with God, if we will pray unto them; very easily may we put this away by many reasons. First, that the cases be not like. For when they were alive, they could know the need of the people: but now who can tell whether they know any thing of our calamities and need? Isaiah saith, Abraham did not know them that were in his age. Again, if the people had come to them to have desired their prayers, as they would have taken this for an admonishment of their duty to the people, so would they again have warned the people of their duty, that with them they also would pray unto God themselves. Whereas there be no such reciprocal and mutual offices between the dead and the living. Now cannot we admonish them, and tell them of our needs; or if we should go about it, surely we should still stand in a doubt, whether they did perceive us or no. But if they did perceive the miseries of their brethren, surely their rest would not be without great grief; and of this we are sure, that they can tell us nothing also. Besides this, this their reasoning smelleth, as it that went before, of man's reason, which is a fool in God's service, and of a good intent which is not according to knowledge. We may not do after that which is good in our own eyes, but according to that which God biddeth us do. In our eyes it seemeth good, that as to kings and great men we use means by men, which are of their privy chambers, or are about them, either to come to their speech, or to attain our suits, so we should do to God by his saints. But to dream on this sort with God, to use saints so, were and is unto faith very foolish: for God useth no such privy chambers to hide himself in. "He is at hand," saith David, "to all that call upon him." And Moses said before him: "God is near thee in all thy prayers. No nation hath their gods so nigh unto them as our God is unto us in all our prayers." He needeth none to put him in remembrance of us; for he hath all things open to his eyes: the height of the hills and the bottom of the depths are in his sight. Nothing can hide itself from his knowledge. He hath ordained Christ Jesus alonely to be the means by whom we shall speed and receive our requests, which be according to his will, if we open our purse-mouth, that he may pour into the same; I mean faith. For as a thing poured upon a vessel or other thing, the mouth being closed, is spilt and lost; so if we ask any thing according to God's will by Christ, the same doth us no good, except the purse-mouth of our hearts be opened by faith to receive it. _{1 Tim. ii.}

But to make an end. St Paul telleth plainly, that without faith prayer is not made. Now in that faith is due only to God, (for cursed is he that hath his faith in man, saint, or angel,) to God only let us make our prayers, but by Jesus Christ, and in his name only; for only in him is the Father well pleased. This if we do, and that often, as Christ willeth, *oportet semper orare,* we must pray always; then shall we undoubtedly in all things be directed by God's holy Spirit, whom Christ hath promised to be our doctor, teacher, and comforter. And therefore need we not to fear what man or devil can do unto us, either by false teaching or cruel persecution: for our pastor is such one, that none can take his sheep out of his hands. To him be praise for ever. Amen. _{Rom. x.} _{Matt. iii. xvii.} _{Luke xviii.} _{John xiv. xv. xvi.} _{Psal. xxvii.} _{John x.}

CHAPTER XIV.

THE KNITTING UP OF THE MATTER, AND CONCLUSION OR PERORATION, WITH THE AUTHOR'S DESIRE AND PRAYER FOR THE PERSECUTED BRETHREN.

AND thus much, my good brethren and sisters, on our dear Lord and Saviour Jesus Christ, I thought good to write unto you for your comfort in these troublesome days, and for the confirmation of the truth that ye have already received: from the which, if you for fear of man, loss of goods, friends, or life, do swerve or depart, you depart and swerve from Christ, and so snare yourself in Satan's sophistry to your utter subversion. Therefore, as Peter saith: "Watch, and be sober: for as a roaring lion he seeketh to devour you." But be ye strong in faith, that is, stagger not, waver _{1 Pet. v.}

<small>Acts ii.
Deut. xx.</small> not in God's promises, and be assured that they pertain unto you, that God is your God, that he is with you in trouble,
<small>Psal. xci.</small> and will deliver you and glorify you. But yet see that ye call upon him, specially that you enter not into temptation,
<small>Matt. xxvi.
Luke xxii.</small> as he taught his disciples to pray, even at such time as he saw Satan desire to sift them, as now he hath desired to sift us. O most dear Saviour, prevent him now, as thou didst then, with thy prayer, we beseech thee, and grant that our faith faint not; but strengthen us to confirm the weak, that they deny not thee and thy gospel, that they return
<small>2 Pet. ii.</small> not to their vomit and puddle of mire in popery and superstition, as massing, praying to saints, praying for the dead, or worshipping the work of men's hands instead of thee their Saviour. Oh, let us not so run down headlong into perdition,
<small>Heb. vi. x.</small> stumbling on those sins, from the which there is no recovery,
<small>Matt. x.
Mark viii.
Luke xi.
Gen. xix.
Matt. xxvii.</small> but a causing of thee to deny us before thy Father, making our latter end worse than the beginning; as chanced to Lot's wife, Judas Iscariot, Franciscus Spira[1] in these our days, and to many others: but rather strengthen us all in thy grace, and in those things which thy word teacheth; that we may here hazard our life for thy sake. And so shall
<small>Matt. xvi.</small> we be sure to save it; as, if we seek to save it, we can but lose it: and it being lost, what profit can we have, if we win the whole world? Oh, set them always before our eyes, not as reason doth this life, or the pleasures of the same, death of the body, prisonment, &c.; but everlasting life, and those unspeakable joys, which undoubtedly they shall have, that take up their cross and follow thee. Set ever before us also the eternal fire, and perpetual destruction of soul and body, that they must needs at length leap into, which are afraid of the hoar-frost of adversity, that man or the devil stirreth up to stop and hinder us from going forward in our journey to heaven's bliss; to the which, O Lord, do thou bring us for thy name's sake. Amen.

Pray for all your brethren which be in prison and exile, and so absent from you in body, but yet present with you

[[1] An eminent lawyer of Citadella near Padua, who embraced, and afterwards renounced, the reformed faith, A. D. 1546. Some account of him may be found in Seckendorf, Hist. Lutheranismi, Lib. III. sect. CXXIX. Vol. II. p. 601, and Sleidan, History of the Reformation, Book XXI.]

in spirit; and heartily pray God once to prove us, and trust us again with his holy word and gospel; that we may be suffered to speak, and you to hear his voice, as heretofore we and you have done, but unthankfully and negligently, I may say, yea, very unworthily and carnally. And therefore is his most just anger fallen now upon us. He remember his mercy towards us in his time, we beseech him! Amen.

Appendix

Keep Thee unto the Word

By R. Magnusson Davis, B.A., LL.B.,
Founder, New Matthew Bible Project.

Keep Thee Unto the Word
Copyright © 2022, April; June, by Ruth Magnusson (Davis)

All rights reserved. This work may not be reproduced in whole or in part in any form (beyond such copying as is permitted by applicable law, and except for reviewers for the public press and excerpts of 200 words or less with credit to the author and citation of this book), without written permission from the publisher.

Contact publisher at www.baruchhousepublishing.com

Scripture quotations are from The October Testament, the New Testament of the New Matthew Bible (NMB), and the 1537/1549 Matthew Bible (MB). Quotations from other Bible versions are for the purposes of comment, criticism, and education only.

Preface ... 117

Part One
Psalm 23. The Word of God as Pasture and Comfort ... 127

Part Two
1 Peter 1:13. The Word Declared to the Soul:
Of Faith, Grace, and Hope ... 155

Part Three
1 Corinthians 13:12. The Sight of the Word ... 179

Part Four
Keeping unto the Word ... 189

Schedule A
John Calvin's commentary on Psalm 23 ... 197

Notes on Schedule A ... 208

Preface

THE PSALM THAT is commonly known now as Psalm 23 was formerly known as Psalm 22. That was the number assigned to it in the Septuagint, the Greek Old Testament used by the early Christian church. In the 4th century, Jerome followed the Septuagint numbering when he made the Latin Vulgate Bible, and then, in 1535, Myles Coverdale also followed it in his English Bible.

Two years later, in 1537 when Coverdale published his treatise on the psalm, he entitled it *A very excellent and swete exposition upon the two and twentye Psalme of David.* (In this appendix I will use the short title *"Sweet Exposition."*) In the treatise, Coverdale continued to employ the traditional reference to the psalm as number 22. As mentioned in the foreword to this volume, he translated this treatise from Martin Luther; however, Luther's full, original title was, *A Paraphrase on the twenty-second Psalm according to the Septuagint Version, or the twenty-third according to the notation of the Hebrew text.*

When John Rogers published the Matthew Bible in 1537, the same year the *Sweet Exposition* was published, he used Coverdale's translation of the psalm but showed it as Psalm 23, as Martin Luther also had done in his German translation of the Bible. Rogers and Luther, like most modern translators, followed the numbering system of the Hebrew Masoretic Text instead of the Septuagint.[1] Both Old Testament texts showed the same number of psalms but spliced or combined them differently, as shown in the following chart:

---

[1] Modern exceptions include the Douay-Rheims Bible, which is based on the Latin Vulgate, and the Orthodox Study Bible, which is translated from the Septuagint.

Greek (Septuagint) numbering	Hebrew (Masoretic) numbering
1-8	1-8
9	9-10
10-112	11-113
113	114-115
114-115	116
116-145	117-146
146-147	147
148-150	148-150

For this book, I retitled Coverdale's treatise *A Sweet Exposition on Psalm 23* in order to be consistent with the Matthew Bible and modern numbering. I should also note that, though I may refer to the *Sweet Exposition* as Coverdale's treatise or work, it was, of course, just as much Luther's, since he was the original author. Luther was a mighty warrior for God's holy word, and his tremendous reverence for the word is manifest in this as much as in all his other works.

MY CUSTOM WHEN discussing English Bible versions is to divide the time from the 16th century to today into three periods, which I have termed the Reformation, Literal, and Modern Periods. I used this division in *The Story of the Matthew Bible* to distinguish the influences that prevailed on Bible translation and revision during these times.

The Reformation Period covers the years from roughly 1525 to 1553, and comprises the latter part of King Henry VIII's reign and the short time that his son, Edward VI, was on the throne. It ended when Mary Tudor, a staunch Roman Catholic, became the queen of England. I call the three complete Bibles produced during this period the Reformation Bibles. They were, first Coverdale's of 1535 (COV), then the 1537 Matthew Bible (MB), and, finally, the Great Bible of 1539-1540 (GRT). These three Bibles contained the excellent translations of just two men, William Tyndale and Myles Coverdale, though altogether Coverdale's contribution was the larger (see Foreword). They manifest God's calling upon the lives of these men, who were friends and sometimes worked together.

A notable influence of the Reformation Period was a greater reverence for antiquity, the primitive church, and patristic teaching and tradition than one often finds in the later periods. This may in some small part explain the new interpretation of Psalm 23 that was introduced in the Geneva Bible. The Geneva notes departed from the traditional understanding that Psalm 23 was written in praise of God's word, as is taught so passionately in the *Sweet Exposition.*

The Literal Period began in 1557 with the publication of the Geneva New Testament, which was a revision of Tyndale's New Testament by the radical Puritan William Whittingham. Soon thereafter, in 1560, came the complete Geneva Bible (GNV). The Old Testament and Apocryphal books of the 1560 GNV were a Puritan revision of Coverdale's Great Bible.[2] I refer

---

[2] I use the word "Puritan" in its true, historic sense. The Oxford English Dictionary (OED) records the first written use of "puritan" in 1565 in a book *Fortresse of Faith*: "We know to weare in the church holy vestements, and to be apparailled priestlike semeth ... absurde to the puritans off our countre, to the zelous gospellers of Geneva." Here "the puritans of our country ... the zealous gospellers of Geneva" means the English Puritans who returned from Geneva after Queen Elizabeth I ascended the throne in 1558. Their mission was to "purify" and "restore" the Church according to their now oft-forgotten, militant vision, and they believed that they were destined to be the preachers and prophets of the restored Church. They melded these ideals together with socio-political goals, and were willing to – and did – use political intrigue, revolution, and the sword to realize their vision. They also used their Bible, the Geneva Bible, to advance their goals, as shown in *The*

to both the GNV and the 1611 King James Version (KJV) as literal Bibles because they were produced during the time that Geneva's literal method of translation guided Bible revision,[3] though other influences also figured prominently during the Literal Period.

The anonymous preface to the 1560 GNV charged that the original Scripture translations of Tyndale and Coverdale "required greatly to be perused and reformed" according to the Puritans' "ripe" understanding and "clear light."[4] It also claimed that their literal translations of Hebrew grammatical idioms (or "Hebrew phrases," as they were then called) corrected Tyndale's and Coverdale's work, and that their method was more reverent and apostolic.[5] However, it cannot be said that

---

Story of the Matthew Bible: Part 2, The Scriptures Then and Now (Canada: Baruch House Publishing, 2021) (hereinafter referred to as *Story Part 2*).

However, Puritanism was already developing well before the 1565 quotation given in the OED. The Puritan influence can be seen in Edmund Becke's 1549 Bible, which was the first Puritan revision of the Matthew Bible (examined in *Story Part 2*). Then, in 1552, Thomas Cranmer's foreword to the Book of Common Prayer addressed Puritan scruples about ceremonies, thus revealing that Puritanism was already raising contentions in the young Church of England at that time. Puritan doctrine was strongly asserted in the 1560 Geneva Bible notes; for example, the notes on the Psalms say musical instruments in worship are "forbidden under the Gospel." Puritanism rooted strongly in England after the "Geneva gospellers" returned to England during Queen Elizabeth's reign, and finally culminated in the Puritan revolution of the 17th century.

[3] See footnotes 5 and 6 to this Preface, below.

[4] In the preface to the 1560 Geneva Bible it was written, "We thought that we should bestow our labours and study in nothing which could be more acceptable to God and conformable to his Church than in the translating of the Holy Scriptures into our native tongue; the which thing, albeit that divers heretofore have endeavoured to achieve [i.e. Tyndale and Coverdale], yet considering the infancy of those times and imperfect knowledge of the tongues, in respect of this ripe age and clear light which God hath now revealed, the translations required greatly to be perused and reformed." The 1560 Geneva preface is reproduced in the modern spelling Tolle Lege edition of the 1599 GNV, beginning at page xxvii.

[5] Concerning literalism, the 1560 GNV preface read, "Now as we have chiefly observed the sense, and labored always to restore it to all integrity: so have we most reverently kept the propriety of the words, considering that the Apostles who

PREFACE

the Reformation Bibles were not literal. They were.[6] In fact, in this Appendix we will see several verses where the more literal translations of the Matthew Bible guarded teaching about the word of God that was lost through non-literal revisions in the Geneva version. After considering these revisions, readers may decide for themselves if they reveal greater light and reverence.

The Modern Period began in 1894 with the publication of the complete Revised Version (RV). I refer to it and all subsequent versions as the modern Bibles. Though scholars often distinguish Bibles of the Modern Period based on the Greek text employed in their translation of the New Testament, in truth a variety of other influences have had far more significant consequences for the doctrine and message of God's word than textual issues. Doctrinal influences include so-called higher criticism, millenarianism, and Christian Zionism.

As to translation method, a notable RV influence on modern Bibles is the transliteration of nouns related to hell and the place of eternal retribution, including *Sheol* and *Hades*. These transliterations, together with new definitions in *Strong's Concordance*, were influenced by non-traditional beliefs of members of the RV revision committee about the doctrine of eternal retribution, and they have changed what some people believe about

---

spake and wrote to the Gentiles in the Greek tongue, rather constrained them to the lively phrase of the Hebrew, than enterprised far by mollifying their language to speak as the Gentiles did. And for this and other causes we have in many places reserved the Hebrew phrases, notwithstanding that they may seem somewhat hard in their ears that are not well practiced." (However, the apostles spoke and wrote in natural idiom, earnestly desiring their message of salvation to be as understandable and clear as possible. This is discussed in in chapters 19-22 of *Story Part 2.*)

[6] One important difference between the translation methods of the Reformation and Literal Periods was that the Geneva and King James revisers added extensive literal translation of Hebrew grammatical idioms to the literal translation of lexical idioms. This is also discussed *Story Part 2*.

the destiny of the human soul after death.[7] Modern Bibles have also adopted various alternate renderings proposed in the RV marginal notes, which affect meaning and doctrine.[8]

IN THE MATTHEW BIBLE, which readers will get to know in this Appendix, the New Testament was the translation of William Tyndale. The first fourteen books of the Old Testament were also his work, while the balance of the Old Testament and the Apocryphal books (except the Prayer of Manneseh) were from Coverdale's 1535 Bible. Therefore, all the MB psalms were Coverdale's translation. A third man, John Rogers, compiled the MB and added notes to explain Hebrew idioms and imagery, historical matters, Protestant doctrine, and more.[9] We will see some of his notes here.

The Matthew Bible entered the stream of English Bibles and became the real, though generally unacknowledged, base of the King James Version when, under King Henry VIII, Coverdale amended it to follow Jerome's Latin translation more closely, and to remove all John Rogers' notes.[10] These changes were in-

---

[7] Many moderns believe there are three possible destinies for the soul after death: heaven, hell (Gehenna), and a third place, Sheol/Hades, which latter is a "waiting place" for all departed spirits. This doctrine may be derived from the notes of the Revised Version of the Bible, and also from Strong's *Concordance*. (James Strong was part of the RV revision project.) Myles Coverdale wrote *The Hope of the Faithful* to defend the traditional doctrine against the Roman Catholics, who had devised purgatory as a third place, and he showed from the Scripture that there is only heaven and hell. *The Hope of the Faithful* is part of the Baruch House series of Coverdale books, published in 2020.

[8] As shown in *Story Part 2*, chapters 24-28.

[9] For more information about the making of the 1537 Matthew Bible, see *The Story of the Matthew Bible: Part 1, That Which We First Received* (Canada: Baruch House Publishing, 2018).

[10] A. S. Herbert, Bible cataloguer and historian, wrote of the Matthew Bible, "This version, which welds together the best work of Tyndale and Coverdale, is generally considered to be the real primary version of our English Bible." Herbert, *Historical*

tended to pacify the conservatives, who missed the old, familiar verses of the Latin Bible. The amended Matthew Bible became known as the Great Bible (GRT). As mentioned, the Great Bible went on to serve as the base for the Geneva revision, except for the New Testament, which was a direct revision of Tyndale's work. The GRT also served as the base for the Bishops' Bible, which was used as the base of the King James Version; however, the KJV was greatly influenced by the Geneva Bible, as will be seen. The KJV then went on to serve as the base for the Revised Version of 1894, which has in turn influenced many modern Bibles. Therefore, the post-Reformation Scripture translations we will see in this Appendix are in reality a succession of revisions that overlaid and progressively altered the original translations of William Tyndale and Myles Coverdale. The process of these revisions is illustrated in the chart below:

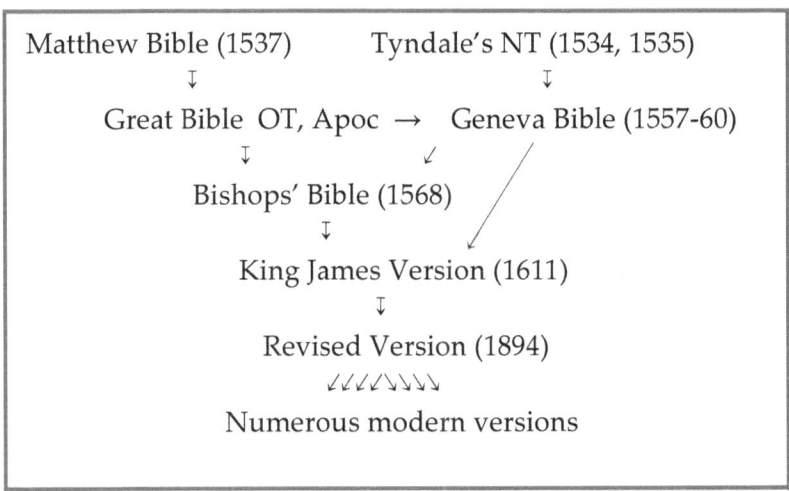

Catalogue of Printed Editions of the English Bible 1525-1961 (New York: The American Bible Society, 1968), 18.

THIS APPENDIX LOOSELY follows the outline of chapter 16 in *The Story of the Matthew Bible: Part 2, The Scriptures Then and Now*. However, it contains much refined and new material, including a comparison of John Calvin's extraordinarily different exposition of Psalm 23 with that of Coverdale and Luther in the *Sweet Exposition*. It also shows how Calvin's new exposition informed the Geneva Bible and has influenced modern versions.

It may surprise some readers to see the great gulf between the teaching of Calvin on the one hand, and that of Coverdale and Luther (with also William Tyndale and John Rogers) on the other hand. This is because their differences are little understood today, except in some Lutheran circles. The reality is that, despite appearances, they were often at odds concerning fundamental questions of biblical interpretation, faith, and practice, including not only the place of music and images in the Church and the Christian duty of obedience to the governing authorities, but also as to the person and divinity of Christ, the meaning and interpretation of Old Testament Messianic prophecies, and the nature of the New Covenant.

To give a clearer sense of the differences – and they are significant – I would refer people to two books. One is a recent English translation of the 16th-century Latin work of Aegidius Hunnius, a Wittenberg theologian. It is entitled *The Judaizing Calvin*. In this short book, Hunnius, quoting from Calvin's Latin commentaries, exposed several ways in which Calvin's expositions of Old Testament Messianic prophecy were more Jewish than Christian. Hunnius showed how Calvin subtly robbed the Messianic prophecies of their essential vigour and effect, and he passionately defended the orthodox doctrine. He concluded in no uncertain terms that Calvin was a false teacher who subtly but gravely undermined the foundations of the faith.

The second book is a record of a 1586 debate between Theodore Beza, who succeeded Calvin as master of the Geneva

PREFACE

Academy, and the Lutheran professor Dr. Jakob Andreae. It is entitled *Lutheranism vs. Calvinism: The Classic Debate at the Colloquy of Montbeliard*. Of particular interest is the discussion concerning the person and divinity of Christ. At the conclusion of the colloquy, Dr. Andreae refused his hand to Beza, no doubt because to do so would be a false show of brotherhood, akin to wishing Godspeed to a false teacher. In this regard, the apostle John wrote:

> **2 John 1:9-11** He who endures in the doctrine of Christ, has both the Father and the Son. If anyone comes to you and does not bring this doctrine, do not receive him into your house, neither bid him Godspeed. For he who bids him Godspeed is partaker of his evil deeds.

The things that we will see in this Appendix clearly reveal the differences between Luther and the early Reformers on the one hand, and Calvin and his followers on the other, so that, in the end, readers will be bound to choose between them. In too many foundational respects their teachings simply cannot be reconciled, and they touch on the doctrines of Christ and his holy word. To whom should we refuse our hand?

These issues must be considered soberly, prayerfully, and fearfully. I have approached this work in that spirit. So that there can be no question of misrepresentation, I give side-by-side comparisons of the teachings of the parties in their own words. It is not a matter of mere opinion, but of proof by showing and contrasting. I did this also in Part 2 of *The Story of the Matthew Bible*, where I contrasted the original Scripture translations of Tyndale and Coverdale with the Calvinist and Puritan revisions in the Geneva Bible. This way readers can plainly see the differences, check my work, understand what was changed, and judge for themselves. With Hunnius's book in hand, I also demonstrated how Calvin's commentaries influenced the revisions to Old Testament Messianic prophecies and the new commentaries in the Geneva Bible.

It will no doubt disturb many good and sincere readers to find that I agree with Aegidius Hunnius that John Calvin, who is so widely praised today, was a false teacher. Indeed, in a very real sense it disturbs me also to write this. I loathe and by nature avoid controversy and dispute. However, I love the truth, and I dare not keep silence concerning what I have learned about the Matthew Bible, about Reformation doctrine, and about what has been changed or suppressed.

Therefore, I ask for a full hearing, and for the opportunity to present the lost and forgotten facts, before people cast my work aside. It is important to understand how Calvin and the early Puritans departed from the doctrines of the Reformation. These departures are not well known today, being buried in history and time; therefore, they must be brought to light again for the recovery of truth – the divine truth that was so well, so fully, and so reverently set forth in the translations and notes of the 1537 Matthew Bible.

R.M.D.

Spring, 2022

1

Psalm 23
The Word of God as Pasture and Comfort

*When it comes to survival,
spiritual food can be the most important kind.*
—*George Gabori, concentration camp survivor,
from* When Evils Were Most Free

PSALM 23 WAS written circa 1000 B.C. Affectionately referred to as the Shepherd's Psalm, it is attributed to David, the shepherd king – from whose loins, as to the flesh, was descended the great Shepherd King, Christ the Son of God, about whom David often spoke prophetically. As seen, Coverdale explained in his *Sweet Exposition* that this psalm especially expresses the "praise and thanks of every Christian heart" for God's "dear and holy word," which word is signified by the green pasture with its fresh water and other shepherdly images.

Below is Coverdale's translation of Psalm 23 as it was taken into the 1537 Matthew Bible, together with John Rogers' notes on it. The notes referred to other Bible verses, and I have shown these, and Roger's further notes on them, in italics. Altogether the notes demonstrate the thoughtfulness of Rogers' commentaries, and also provide readers with a taste of the reverence and high regard for God's word that characterized the Matthew Bible throughout it pages:

Psalm 23, Matthew Bible (MB)

1 The Lord is my shepherd; I can want nothing.

2 He feedeth me in a green pasture, and leadeth me to a *fresh water.

3 He quickeneth my soul, and bringeth me forth in the way of righteousness for his name's sake.

4 Though I should walk now in the valley of the *shadow of death, yet I fear no evil, for thou art with me; thy staff and thy sheep-hook comfort me.

5 Thou preparest a *table before me [in the presence of] mine enemies; thou annointest my head with oil, and fillest my cup full.

6 O let thy lovingkindness and mercy follow me all the days of my life, that I may dwell in the house of the Lord forever.

MB notes on Psalm 23 (minimally updated):

v2 note This fresh water is the healthful water of the word of God, of which is spoken at Isaiah 55.

[*Isaiah 55:1 Come to the ⁽ᵃ⁾waters of life, all ye that be thirsty, and ye that have no money. Come, buy, so that ye may have to eat. Come, buy ⁽ᵇ⁾wine and milk without any money or money's worth.*

Note (a) Of these waters ye have in Psalm 23:2.

Note (b) The word of God is called wine and milk: wine because it rejoiceth the heart, in that it pacifieth the conscience and setteth it at rest; milk because it nourisheth and buildeth up the little ones and young ones in the faith, as ye have in 1 Peter 2:2 ("And as newborn babes, desire the milk," etc.)]

v4 note "Shadow" for darkness and affliction.

v5 note Look in Psalm 78.

1. PSALM 23: THE WORD OF GOD AS PASTURE AND COMFORT

> [*Psalm 78:19 For they spoke against God and said, Yea, yea, God shall prepare a ^(a)table in the wilderness, shall he?*
>
> *Note (a) By the table is understood all sorts of victuals necessary for man, yet it is often taken for the bread and water of the wisdom of the word of God, as in Psalm 23:5.*]

In their singular focus on God's word, Rogers' notes agree in spirit entirely with Coverdale's *Sweet Exposition*. They show that he shared Coverdale's interpretation of Psalm 23 – and, of course, Martin Luther's, from whom Coverdale translated the *Exposition*. Nor were the focus and interpretation of these men anything new. Theirs was the traditional understanding. The early church also found in this psalm prophecies and figures of the word, with more or less emphasis on the sacraments. Cyril of Alexandria wrote in the 5th century, "The place of verdure [green pasture] means the ever-fresh words of Holy Scripture, which nourishes the hearts of believers and gives them spiritual strength." Thus God by his word – spoken, written, and sacramental – comforts, builds up, teaches, guides, and sustains those who trust in it and in him.

The traditional understanding of Psalm 23, therefore, had two aspects. The first was that David was praising God as the heavenly shepherd who is always with his sheep to care for and defend them in this present life. Second, in its spiritual aspect, he was in particular praising God's word as the chief and greatest benefit to the sheep; indeed, it is their very life. As Coverdale put it, "This same noble treasure doth holy David praise and extol marvellous excellently."

However, in the 1560 Geneva Bible, the Puritan revisers changed both the translation and interpretation of the psalm to remove the second or spiritual aspect, the praise of God's word as the sheep's chief blessing. God was still praised as the good shepherd, but only as a provider of temporal needs, comforts, and rest. In verse 2, in place of the imagery of food and drink that signified the nourishing function of the word, there was new imagery signifying rest and tranquillity. With this and the new notes, the GNV defeated the traditional understanding of Psalm 23 and Luther's and Coverdale's teaching in the *Sweet Exposition*, not to mention also Rogers' teaching in the Matthew Bible. The Geneva revision of Psalm 23, which will be more familiar to modern readers, and the new teaching in the GNV notes, were as follows:

Psalm 23, 1560/99 Geneva Bible (GNV)

1 The Lord is my shepherd, (a)I shall not want.

2 He maketh me to rest in green pasture, and leadeth me by the still waters.

3 He (a)restoreth my soul, and leadeth me in the (b)paths of righteousness for his name's sake.

4 Yea, though I should walk through the valley of the (a)shadow of death, I will fear no evil, for thou art with me: thy rod and thy staff, they comfort me.

5 Thou dost prepare a (a)table before me in the sight of mine adversaries: thou dost (b)anoint mine head with oil, and my cup runneth over.

6 Doubtless kindness and mercy shall follow me all the days of my life, and I shall remain a long season in the (a)house of the Lord.

GNV notes

v1 note (a) He hath care over me and ministreth unto me all things.

v3 note (a) He comforteth or refresheth me.

v3 note (b) Plain, or straight ways.

1. PSALM 23: THE WORD OF GOD AS PASTURE AND COMFORT

v4 note (a) Though he were in danger of death, as the sheep that wandereth in the dark valley without his shepherd.

v5 note (a) Albeit his enemies sought to destroy him, yet God delivereth him, and dealeth most liberally with him in despite of them.

v5 note (b) As was the manner of great feasts.

v6 note (a) He setteth not his felicities in the pleasures of this world, but in the fear and service of God.

While at first glance there may appear to be little objectionable in the GNV notes, a closer examination reveals problems. For one thing, the note on verse 4 misrepresents David's intent. Nowhere in this psalm did he mean to suggest any similitude of a sheep without his shepherd, much less that the danger of death indicates a sheep without his shepherd. The real message is the opposite: the heavenly shepherd is with his sheep in the midst of all evils, including death, and in every dark valley.

But what the notes do *not* say is also a problem. They say nothing about God's word. This omission and the new translation together bring different doctrine, the significance of which cannot be overstated.

Comparison of treatments of verse 2

Coverdale's translation of Psalm 23 assisted the reader (or hearer) to perceive that God's word as the saints' pasture and drink is a main focus, especially through the imagery of feeding and fresh water in verse 2. Rogers' note then explained plainly that the water signifies the "healthful" word of God. He additionally referred readers to Isaiah 55:1, which speaks of God's word as wine, milk, and the waters of life.

The Geneva Bible, however, intentionally departed from this interpretation. We know that the Puritan revisers were familiar with the Reformation Bibles, which they criticized as lacking light, etc.[1] Also, for their revisions they worked from Psalm 23 in the Great Bible,[2] which, as will be seen, retained the traditional imagery. Therefore, their departure was deliberate, and their omission of all mention of God's word as the pasture and refreshment of the sheep was intentional.

In verse 2, the GNV revision of the verb "feedeth" to "maketh to rest" indicates a shepherd who leads his sheep, not to food, but to rest. Coverdale did write in the *Exposition*, "The word [David] here useth may be called lying or resting, as a beast lieth and resteth upon his four feet" (p.38), so it appears that there is room for a variety of interpretations. I heard a Jewish rabbi expound the Hebrew word as indicating an animal "sprawled on all fours." In the circumstances, and given the ambiguity, the Geneva revisers could have related the "rest" of verse 2 to the peace the sheep receive from God's word, but they chose to put no note on verse 2 and leave their readers with imagery of worldly rest only. They also changed "fresh water," which indicates a quality of drinking water for nourishment, to "still waters," reinforcing the idea of tranquillity and restfulness. Indeed, they adopted an interpretation of Psalm 23 that agrees with the rabbinical expositions I have heard, which emphasize God's care for his people *without* the word – without any consideration of it, nor understanding of how it ministers to the saints, but consistent with the long-held Jewish hope for temporal rest and prosperity.

The Geneva influence (or, perhaps, the Judaic influence) on modern scholarship can be seen in *Wilson's Dictionary of Bible*

---

[1] See notes 4 and 5 to the Preface to this Appendix at pages 120-121.
[2] See the Preface to this Appendix, page 123.

Types. I checked under "pasture," where Wilson wrote with reference to Psalm 23:2, "This beautifully presents to us the precious truth that God's dear people are made to rest and enjoy his rich provision, his supply, and his goodness. God's sheep receive of God's best."[3] However, Wilson did not mention God's word as his best.

John Calvin's influence

The new Puritan teaching can be traced back to John Calvin, who oversaw the preparation of the 1560 Geneva Bible. For Calvin, Psalm 23 spoke nothing about the spiritual riches of the word, but only about worldly riches and provision. His full commentary on Psalm 23 is attached as Schedule A to this Appendix. In the following discussion I will give excerpts from it, and readers may consult the full commentary for context. The numbers in brackets, following a reference to or quotation from Calvin's commentary, refer to the applicable subparagraph in Schedule A.

In his exposition on Psalm 23, when Calvin discussed the imagery of verse 2, he passed over the traditional interpretation, that it signified God's word as the pasture of the sheep. He even suggested that the Hebrew might indicate not a pasture, but shepherds' lodges or cots, being structures where shepherds find shelter from the sun (2.1). However, he also referred to these structures as "sheep-cots" where the sheep are sheltered. His comments are ambiguous, but seem to suggest that whole herds of sheep and lambs sheltered in the cots; but again, he referred only to David alone being sheltered there:

---

[3] Walter Lewis Wilson, *Wilson's Dictionary of Bible Types* (Grand Rapids, Michigan: Eerdmans Publishing Co, 1957), s.v. "Pasture."

Calvin: Some, instead of translating the word נאות, *neoth*, which we have rendered pastures, render it shepherds' cots or lodges. If this translation is considered preferable, the meaning of the Psalmist will be that sheep-cots were prepared in rich pasture grounds, under which he might be protected from the heat of the sun.... He, therefore, compares the great abundance of all things requisite for the purposes of this present life which he enjoyed to meadows richly covered with grass, and to gently flowing streams of water; or he compares the benefit or advantage of such things to sheep-cots; for it would not have been enough to have been fed and satisfied in rich pasture, had there not also being provided waters to drink, and the shadow of the sheep-cot to cool and refresh him. (2.1, 2.4)

Thus Calvin related verse 2 only to the temporal needs of the sheep (or, perhaps, of the shepherd).

Curiously, Calvin indicated that in verse 2 the Geneva Bible rendered the word *neoth* in the plural, as "pastures." However, both the 1560 and 1599 editions of the GNV retained the singular form, though it changed "a green pasture," as it was in the Great Bible, to "green pasture," a non-specific mass noun. It was the KJV which first revised to the plural form, "pastures." This made it even more difficult to perceive that God's word as the one, singular pasture of the sheep was in view.

Wealth vs. the word to draw nearer to God

But the emphasis on temporal benefits was more marked in Calvin's commentary than in the notes of the Geneva Bible – astonishingly and extravagantly so. As will be seen, Calvin advanced David as a kingly model of how to properly enjoy "splendid riches and honours," and all the "royal wealth," "princely pleasures," and "delicacies" that God "fed" him.

1. PSALM 23: THE WORD OF GOD AS PASTURE AND COMFORT

To begin with, in his commentary on Psalm 23, Calvin taught that it is by worldly riches and benefits that God "allures" man to himself – and the greater the riches, the greater the allurement. He did not say that God calls man by his word or by the gospel. Neither did he mention that the devil allures us with riches and pleasures. He taught, rather, that it was not God's word, but David's wealth, pleasures, and abundance which were as "ladders" that helped David "ascend nearer" to God in heaven, and which assisted him to "live to God." And thus did Calvin, who is so widely praised as a champion of God's word, put the use and benefits of worldly things in the place of the use and benefits of the word. He repeatedly emphasized this new doctrine; indeed, he began, filled, and ended his commentary with teaching to this effect:

Calvin:
God, *by his benefits, gently allures us to himself,* as it were by a taste of his fatherly sweetness. (1.1)

[W]e ought the more carefully to mark the example which is here set before us by David, who, elevated to the dignity of sovereign power, surrounded with the splendor of riches and honours, possessed of the greatest abundance of temporal good things, and in the midst of princely pleasures, not only testifies that he is mindful of God, but calling to remembrance the benefits which God has conferred upon him, *makes them ladders by which he may ascend nearer to Him.* (1.2)

[H]e valued all the comforts of the flesh only in proportion as they served to enable him to live to God. He plainly affirms that the end which he contemplated in all the benefits which God had conferred upon him was, that he might dwell in the house of the Lord. (6.5)

> It is, therefore, certain that the mind of David, by the aid of the temporal prosperity which he enjoyed, was elevated to the hope of the everlasting inheritance. (6.6)

Thus Calvin taught that riches and worldly benefits are where we taste the "sweetness" of God, and not in his word. He taught that David ascended to God through his riches, and not by the word. He taught that abundant comforts of the flesh enabled David to live to God and dwell in his house, and not that he treasured the word of God set forth in his house, as Luther frequently wrote. Calvin also taught that it was temporal prosperity which elevated David's mind to the eternal hope, and not God's word. One wonders how the apostle Paul, bound and naked in prison, found the means to elevate his mind to the divine heights that are evident in the prison epistles.

But Calvin gave us no reason to seek in the word for the knowledge of God, nor for the heights of God, nor for the sweetness of God, nor for anything. He taught, rather, to welcome riches to attain to heaven – and this even though Jesus said it is easier for a camel to go through the eye of a needle than for a rich man to enter into heaven (M't. 19:24). Further, in no place did Calvin confess that Jesus Christ is the way, the truth, and the life, and that no one comes to the Father except by him (Joh. 14:6). Contrast Luther, who wrote of Christ that "he who believes in him has all his blessings, and ascends to the Father through him."[4] Indeed, Calvin did not mention Jesus even once in his long commentary on Psalm 23 – a complete departure from the *Sweet Exposition*, in which Christ was frequently men-

---

[4] Martin Luther, "Catholic Epistles," Vol. 30, *Luther's Works*, American Edition (Saint Louis: Concordia Publishing House, 1964), 39.

tioned. Calvin in effect taught intimacy with God apart from Christ and apart from the word, just as the rabbis do.

Therefore, Calvin's teaching on Psalm 23 effectively opposed that of the *Sweet Exposition*, and of Coverdale and Luther. This opposition was not, however, by open disagreement, but by deflection and omission. As a result, and because the traditional interpretation of Psalm 23 has been lost, few are aware of it. But a simple comparison with a short excerpt from the *Sweet Exposition* reveals a completely different spirit:

> **Coverdale:** This lesson should we learn also; namely, to let the world boast of their great riches, honour, power, etc. For these are insecure, uncertain, and transitory wares ... But to his children, as David says here, he gives the right treasure. Therefore we should not, as the dear children and heirs of God, boast about our wisdom, strength, or riches, but of this: that we have the precious pearl, even that worthy word, whereby we know God our loving father, and Jesus Christ whom he has sent. (See page 36. Lightly updated)

Here is manifest not only Coverdale's focus on Christ and his word, but also his disregard for transitory and uncertain worldly riches. To be sure, Calvin suggested twice in his commentary that worldly goods are uncertain things (6.3, 6.5). However, from this we ought to conclude that they are also uncertain ladders, unlike the sure word of God. Calvin also said that David did not "depend upon outward things," which suggests – and rightly so – that worldly goods are not dependable ladders. He also commented that David's thoughts were not "confined" to earthly pleasures (6.4), but he did not say to what extent David thought about, or should have been, thinking about them. He did, however, assert that rich men ought to have a certain "taste or relish" for their earthly blessings (6.1).

Of course, it goes without saying that we ought to be grateful for God's temporal provision for us, and should feel free to enjoy the good things he gives. However, Calvin's emphasis on abundance and princely pleasures was pernicious, and all the more so because he never spoke about enjoying or being grateful for God's word. Indeed, he mentioned the word only once in his long commentary. This mention was not only without any expression of praise or gratitude, it was the odd comment that David's faith remained "shut up in the word of God" when all earthly help failed. Calvin gave a vague nod here also to God's "promise":

> **Calvin:** [David] sufficiently testified that he did not depend upon outward things, nor measured the grace of God according to the judgement of the flesh, but that even when assistance from every earthly quarter failed him, his faith continued shut up in the word of God. Although, therefore, experience led him to hope well, yet it was principally on the promise by which God confirms his people with respect to the future that he depended. (6.2)

Again, despite how it may appear on a superficial reading, this commentary is problematic. For one thing, Calvin suggests David relied foremost on help from "every earthly quarter" until such a time as it failed. Contrast Luther, who wrote in his commentary on Psalm 46, "No power, might, or protection which can comfort, or upon which one can rely, may be sought in the world. Wholly in God, and in God alone, must help be sought." Second, Calvin says the promises David depended on were "with respect to the future." This does not portray a shepherd who is with his sheep here and now. It therefore contradicts the chief assurance of the psalm, not to mention other statements in Calvin's commentary. Further, the apostle Paul used the word "shut up" in Galatians 3:23 with respect to the law, in contradistinction to the faith of the gospel. He wrote, "Before faith came, we were kept and shut up under the law, with a view to the faith that would afterward be declared." It is inappropriate and subtly pejorative to speak of the faith that redeems us from under the law as "shut up." (Of course, Calvin did not write in English. I quote from the widely accepted translation and assume the translator chose his words with knowlegde and care.)

Finally, it is instructive to contrast Calvin's doctrine, that worldly riches assist us to ascend to God, with what the apostle Paul taught about the immediate presence of God by his word:

> **Romans 10:6-8, NMB** The righteousness that comes by faith speaks this way: Say not in your heart, who shall ascend into heaven? (which is nothing else than to fetch Christ down), or, who shall descend into the deep? (which is nothing else than to fetch Christ up from death). But what does the Scripture say? The word is near you, even in your mouth and in your heart. This word is the word of faith that we preach.

Of course, we may properly speak about lifting up our minds to God, or prayers that ascend to God, and so forth. But the general tenor of Calvin's teaching, which we will see again later, was to portray God as distant from us, without any mention of his word as the means by which we may know him here and now – and as if Christ is not himself Emmanuel, God with us.

Looking to riches vs. Looking to the word

Calvin portrayed David, not as a lover and follower of God's word, but as a pious rich man who knew how to make heavenly ladders out of money, and who dutifully expressed an "ardent" gratitude for wealth:

> **Calvin:** David, therefore, by his own example, admonishes the rich of their duty, that they may be the more

ardent in the expression of their gratitude to God, the more delicately he feeds them. (5.4)

For Calvin, therefore, Psalm 23 was all about David's dutiful gratitude to God for the riches that God had delicately fed him (in lieu of feeding him by the word). "Delicately" means "(a) In a way that gratifies the senses, *esp* the sense of taste; luxuriously, sumptuously. Also: in a way that satisfies discriminating or particular requirements; fastidiously, fussily; (b) In an indulgent or pampering manner; softly, indulgently."[5] And so, Calvin taught, the more delicately God "feeds" us, the more ardent our gratitude ought to be. "Ardent" means "glowing with passion, animated by keen desire; intensely eager, zealous, fervent, fervid."[6]

But contrast Coverdale's starkly different teaching. So little did he esteem delicacies, worldly honours, or riches, he wrote in the *Exposition* that they are God's "draff and swillings, with which he fills the hogs' bellies, whom he is disposed to kill." However, to his children God gives the real treasure – his word – for which we should be "heartily" grateful:

> **Coverdale:** May the God of mercy grant us grace so that we also, after the example of David, Paul, and other holy men, may count our treasure, which is even the same that they had, as great, and may magnify it above all the goods upon earth, and heartily give God thanks for it, that he has deigned to give it to us above many thousands of others. (Page 37. Gently updated)

---

[5] Oxford English Dictionary online, s.v. "delicately," entries 1.a and 1.b. A quotation from 1576: "You have received me honourably, sumptuously, and delicately."
[6] Ibid., s.v. "ardent," entry 5. Again, Calvin did not write in English. We assume the competence of his translator.

1. PSALM 23: THE WORD OF GOD AS PASTURE AND COMFORT

Thus, whether rich or poor, whether king or pauper, all who have and believe God's word are equally rich, and may be equally grateful for their treasure. But by making temporal riches the proper object of man's gratitude and affection – even religious affection – Calvin not only made idols of them, he put a false distinction between the worldly rich and the poor. Further, by presenting temporal riches as food from God, he scorned the holy bread of the word.

Omissions and counterfeits in Calvin's commentary

With all Calvin's discussion about how riches should be used and enjoyed, there were two important things he did not say. First, he failed to warn against covetousness, and second, he failed to mention the Christian duty of charity toward the poor. Because it is so easy to overlook what is missing from a text or teaching, I did not become conscious of these omissions until I was reading Coverdale and Luther, and also that great teacher of the early Church, John Chrysostom, on other matters. Again, to compare their teaching with Calvin's reveals their different spirit.

As to covetousness, where Calvin taught an ardent gratitude for delicacies and wealth (e.g. 1.3, 5.4), Coverdale warned:

> **Coverdale:** Let covetousness blind no man. Let the desire of temporal goods possess and rule no man's heart: for out of covetousness, the root of all vice, grows nothing but treason and despair. No righteousness, no fidelity, no truth, no honesty, can be in that heart where greedy covetousness has taken root. Judas, for very greediness of money, gives over God and all love; and he who before was a fellow and companion of the holy congregation of

God's children is become a mate, companion, and leader of the wicked and unbelievers.[7]

And, of course, the Lord Jesus cautioned, "Take heed, and beware of covetousness. For no man's life stands in the abundance of the things that he possesses" (Lu. 12:15). Paul taught that covetousness is a form of idolatry and the root of all evil (Eph. 5:5, Col. 3:5, 1Ti. 6:10).

But Calvin did not warn against covetousness. Further, for the sin of coveting riches he substituted the counterfeit sin of ingratitude for riches, and taught that *not* to have a certain "relish" for them demonstrates ingratitude (6.1). He also said, not only that we should be grateful for God's provision for our needs, which is reasonable, but that we should be more grateful when he gives us *more* than we need (5.4); again, a pernicious concept. He said it is lawful for rich men to enjoy their abundance with a "larger scope" than the common people, so long as, like David, they regulated themselves in the midst of their abundant delicacies (5.6). Thus, along with his great, swelling words of humility and restraint, Calvin in effect fostered covetousness.

Contrast again Luther, who wrote that we must "deal with temporal goods as if they did not belong to us. We must limit our enjoyment of them to what is necessary for the preservation of the body. With the rest we must help our neighbour."[8] Thus when we have more than we need, it is our duty to use it to help others, and for doing good – for helping those in need, including the common people.

---

[7] Myles Coverdale, *Fruitful Lessons upon the Passion, Burial, Resurrection, Ascension, and of the Sending of the Holy Ghost* (British Columbia, Canada: Baruch House Publishing, 2021), 80. Gently updated.

[8] Martin Luther, "Catholic Epistles," Vol. 30, *Luther's Works*, 35.

1. PSALM 23: THE WORD OF GOD AS PASTURE AND COMFORT

On the duty of charity, John Chrysostom wrote, "he is of all men to be most pitied, who lives in luxury without sharing his wealth with others."[9] Psalm 41:1 reads, "Blessed is he who considers the poor: the Lord shall deliver him in the time of trouble." Luther wrote that to neglect the poor is effectively to rob them:

> **Luther:** Over and beyond that pride and idolatry [of riches], the flesh adds theft and rapine; namely, when it does not follow the example of Job and does not share its possessions with the poor, does not clothe the naked, and does not perform other duties of love. For the flesh loves and watches over its riches to such an extent that not even the rich themselves enjoy them. First, therefore, the rich become idolaters contrary to the first table. Secondly, they become unrighteous toward their neighbour, robbers and thieves; for they should give to the poor yet do not give.... The common danger for rich people is the sin of omission, when they do not come to the aid of the poor and needy, even though God has sternly commanded, "Share your bread with the hungry, and bring the homeless poor into your house" (Isa. 58:17).[10]

But Calvin allowed this sin of omission. He never once mentioned the duty of the rich to share with the poor. In fact, he rather emphasized that it was lawful for rich people to enjoy their wealth apart from poor people – who, he callously said, offend if they are ungrateful for their "coarse loaf" (5.4). While Luther emphasized that love requires the rich to assist those who have

---

[9] John Chrysostom, *Four Discourses of Chrysostom, Chiefly on the Parable of the Rich Man and Lazarus,* trans. F. Allen, London: Longmans, Green, Reader, and Dyer, 1869 (facsimile; Kessinger Publishing, USA, no date), 59.
[10] Martin Luther, "Lectures on Genesis," Vol. 4, *Luther's Works,* 381.

but a coarse loaf, and that the rich are "sternly commanded" to provide food and shelter to the poor and homeless, Calvin's command to the rich was to merely moderate their enjoyment of their abundance (5.5) – and never mind the commoners; let them be grateful for their coarse loaves.

It is tiresome to unravel this web of subtleties. What does the Scripture say?

> **Colossians 3:1-5, 16, NMB.** If you then are risen again with Christ, seek those things that are above, where Christ sits on the right hand of God. Set your affection on things that are above, and not on things which are on the earth. For you are dead, and your life is hid with Christ in God. When Christ who is our life shows himself, then shall you also appear with him in glory. Mortify therefore your members which are on the earth: fornication, uncleanness, unnatural desire, evil desire, and covetousness, which is the worshipping of idols.... Let the word of Christ dwell in you plenteously in all wisdom.

But Calvin taught us to set our affection on the things that are below, and to let gratitude for riches dwell ardently in us – albeit with moderated relish, an absurd contradiction. However, God's true people lay aside their old self (Eph. 4:22-24), and, walking by the Holy Spirit in the new life, they do not fulfil the lusts of the flesh (Gal. 5:16, 25). Their treasure is God's word.

Psalm 23:3. The righteous way vs. easy paths

The Geneva Bible revisions to verse 3 of Psalm 23 also manifest Calvin's doctrine. The change from the concept of quickening the soul, as if to new life, to that of restoring it, as if to a former state, is directly from him. So also is the GNV note describing the paths of righteousness as "plain or straight." In the 16th century "plain" meant "level," so the picture portrayed in the

GNV is one of paths that are easy to traverse. This was Calvin's teaching, as will be seen.

Below are compared again the MB and GNV (the MB had no note on this verse):

Psalm 23, verse 3

MB He quickeneth my soul, and bringeth me forth in the way of righteousness for his name's sake.

GNV He ⁽¹⁾restoreth my soul, and leadeth me in the ⁽²⁾paths of righteousness for his name's sake.

GNV note (1) He comforteth or refresheth me.

GNV note (2) Plain, or straight ways.

The MB translation, "He quickeneth my soul," indicates the life-quickening work of God's word in a believer's soul in the power of the Holy Spirit. In the 16th century, the word "quickeneth" could take stronger force than it does now, meaning to give or raise up to very life. Therefore, it indicates the new birth and new life of righteousness that accompanies conversion and salvation (as well as the spiritual and moral rejuvenation that believers regularly experience from hearing God's word). This meaning is reinforced by the next phrase, "bringeth me forth in the way of righteousness." To "bring forth" means to give birth to, or bring into being.[11]

Thus the implicit understanding of verse 3 in the MB is that God quickens the human soul to new life – his divine life – then to walk in the new way of righteousness. In a note on Psalm 1 in the MB, Rogers explained, "*Way* in the scriptures is taken for

---

[11] OED online, s.v. "bring," verb, entry 1 under Phrasal Verbs: "To bring forth: 1. To produce, give birth to, bring into being, bear, yield (offspring; fruit, flowers, etc.; natural products; products, effects, results.)"

whatsoever we do or go about, be it good or evil." This quickening, or conversion to the new way, comes about through hearing the word of God in the power of the Holy Spirit.

St. Augustine translated verse 3, "He has converted my soul: He has led me forth in the paths of righteousness, for His Name's sake." In his exposition on this verse, Augustine wrote, "He has brought me forth in the narrow ways, wherein few walk, of his righteousness; not for my merit's sake, but for his name's sake."[12] This signifies the narrow and difficult way that leads to eternal life, of which Jesus spoke (M't 7:12-14), and which follows conversion and the new birth. Again, this conversion means turning from one direction, or way, to a new and different way.

However, the GNV speaks of "restoring the soul." Restoration involves returning to, or being restored to, a former way. It tacitly, therefore, excludes the idea of conversion. And then, instead of "bringing forth" in paths of righteousness, the GNV speaks only of "leading," which is consistent with the concept of guidance along existing paths. That God by his word and Holy Spirit leads us is of course true, and in itself this change might not be considered significant; however, given the context, the GNV robbed the concept of conversion and the new Christian way of life from the psalm.

These GNV revisions followed Calvin, who, in his commentary on Psalm 23, blurred critical semantic distinctions. First, he said the words *restoration, make anew, recover,* and *conversion* (or *quicken to life; bring forth*) all mean the same thing, and they all

---

[12] Saint Augustine, Bishop of Hippo, "Expositions on the Book of Psalms," editor A. Cleveland Cox, in *The Nicene and Post-Nicene Fathers,* First Series, Vol. VIII (Grand Rapids, Michigan: Wm. B. Eerdmans Publishing Company, 1974), 60.

1. PSALM 23: THE WORD OF GOD AS PASTURE AND COMFORT

refer merely to recovery from weakness or disease. But at the same time, he incongruously admitted that "conversion," not "restoration," was the literal meaning of the Hebrew:

> **Calvin:** As it is the duty of a good shepherd to cherish his sheep, and when they are diseased or weak to nurse and support them, David declares that this was the manner in which he was treated by God. The restoring of the soul, as we have translated it, or the conversion of the soul as it is literally rendered, is of the same import as to make anew, or to recover (3.1).

Calvin thus justified the non-literal rendering by saying it means the same as the literal rendering, which it does not.

Calvin also defeated the traditional teaching about the paths of righteousness by denying that they have anything to do with the guidance of the Holy Spirit – or, indeed, with anything spiritual. He even denied that they have anything to do with righteousness, but strangely indicated that the paths of righteousness have only to do with "the maintenance of this present life" in the limited, worldly senses of bodily provision and defence. He also asserted that they are "easy" paths, and that those who walk in them are "at ease" (again, "plain" means "level" here):

> **Calvin:** By the paths of righteousness, he means easy and plain paths. As he still continues his metaphor, *it would be out of place to understand this as referring to the direction of the Holy Spirit*. He has stated a little before that God liberally supplies him with all that is requisite for the maintenance of the present life, and now he adds, that he is defended by him from all trouble. The amount of what is said is, that God is in no respect wanting to his people, seeing he sustains them by his power, invigorates and quickens them, and averts from them whatever is hurt-

ful, *that they may walk at ease in plain and straight paths* (3.2).

What Calvin meant by "quicken" here is not clear, except, as he carefully pointed out, it has nothing to do with the Holy Spirit.

The foregoing shows that Calvin was the source of the GNV redefinition of paths of righteousness as easy – as unspiritual, easy, and straight: not "strait" – that is, not narrow and difficult, as Jesus taught (M't. 7:14. Note too, Coverdale wrote that "worldly men" consider the strait way an easy one [p. 65], and that the pope made the strait way wide [p. 103]). Calvin also taught paths that have nothing to do with the Holy Spirit, nor with God's word: paths of righteousness which are not, in fact, paths of righteousness. He thus robbed the precious truth that God brings us forth into a new way, wherein we endeavour to walk in heavenly righteousness by the power of the Holy Spirit.

Psalm 23:5. The table of swine

Calvin's comments on verse 5 of Psalm 23 warrant mention. This verse concerns the table that God sets before us in the presence of our enemies. Calvin taught that it is lawful for the wealthy to enjoy the delicacies of their abundant table – their table set with riches and comforts – so long as they do not become "dissolved in voluptuous pleasure," like swine who stuff themselves. He wrote:

> **Calvin:** Not that it is unlawful for rich men to enjoy more freely the abundance which they possess than if God had given them a smaller portion; but all men ought to beware, (and much more kings,) lest they should be dissolved in voluptuous pleasures. David, no doubt, as was perfectly lawful, allowed himself larger scope than if he had been only one of the common people, or than if he had still dwelt in his father's cottage, but he so regulated

himself in the midst of his delicacies, as not at all to take pleasure in stuffing and fattening the body. He knew well how to distinguish between the table which God had prepared for him and a trough for swine. (5.6)

Thus Calvin's teaching is that, for David and self-regulating "rich men" like him, worldly delicacies and abundance are the holy table God has set before them. However, he insinuated that for others this same table is a "trough for swine." He may have revealed where he found his holy table, but we ought to have no doubt that David supped at another table, a truly holy one, with Luther, Coverdale, Rogers, Cyril, Augustine, and all who love God's word in spirit and truth.

The true ladder taught in Scripture

I make a final observation concerns Calvin's concept of using riches as ladders to ascend to God. (Some additional criticisms of Calvin's commentary are discussed in the concluding Notes to Schedule A, beginning at page 208.)

Calvin's teaching about ladders obscures an important biblical passage. In Genesis 28, Moses described a significant dream that the patriarch Jacob had about a ladder that "reached to heaven," and on which the angels were seen ascending and descending. This is the only place in the entire Bible that mentions a ladder, so Calvin's reference to ladders that ascend to God will naturally put readers in mind of Jacob's dream. But, what did Jacob's dream mean?

The anciently-held opinion, as Luther explained it, is that Jacob's ladder was a figure of Christ and his Incarnation. It is by this holy and sacred ladder that man ascends to God, and where God meets with man. Also, the angels, delighted by the Incarnation, ascend and descend the ladder in joy and in the service of the Lord.[13] As I understand the Scripture, the Lord Jesus himself alluded to this figure when he said to Nathanael:

> **John 1:50-51, NMB** Because I said to you, I saw you under the fig tree, you believe. You will see greater things than these...Truly truly I say to you, hereafter you shall see heaven open, and the angels of God ascending and descending over the Son of man.

Therefore, it is by this divine ladder, by the Lord Jesus himself, that man ascends to God. But Calvin compromised the biblical reference. Not only did he do this by teaching another and a different ladder, one that excluded Christ, he also again made plural that which should be singular, since the Scripture speaks of only one ladder. (We have seen how Calvin did a similar thing with pasture[s], and will see later how he did it with grace[s].) Clearly, there is a great gulf between Luther's Christ-centered teaching about the one, holy ladder to heaven, and Calvin's many ladders of riches and pleasures.

Overview from Old English to today

It is instructive to see the history of the translations of verse 2 of Psalm 23. All the pre-1560 English translations employed imagery of nourishing or feeding. Even in the pre-Wycliffite, Old English and West Midlands versions, in original spelling below, the references to "norissed me" and "fedde me" are plain:

Psalm 23:1-2 in English translations before 1560

Old English Drihten me raet, ne byth me nanes godes wan. And he me geset on swythe good feohland. And fedde me be waetera stathum.

---

[13] See Martin Luther, "Lectures on Genesis," *Luther's Works,* Vol. 5, 212f, where it is mentioned that Ambrose, Bernard, and Augustine, also held this view.

1. PSALM 23: THE WORD OF GOD AS PASTURE AND COMFORT

> **West Midlands Psalter, c 1350** Our Lord gouerneth me, and nothing shal defailen to me. In the sted of pastur he sett me ther. He norissed me upon water of fyllyng.
>
> **Wycliffe, 1380** The Lord governeth me, and nothing shall fail to me. In the place of pasture there he hath set me. He nourished me on the water of refreshing.
>
> **COV & MB** The Lord is my shepherd; I can want nothing. He feedeth me in a green pasture, and leadeth me to a fresh water.
>
> **GRT** The Lord is my shepherd, therefore can I lack nothing. He shall feed me in a green pasture, and lead me forth beside the waters of comfort.

Coverdale's revision to "waters of comfort" in the Great Bible clearly signifies God's word as our refreshment in adversity. Formerly, the word "comfort" had broader meaning than it does now, including to strengthen morally or bodily, to assist, and to support, as well as to soothe in grief or trouble (which last is the chief modern sense). Therefore, when Coverdale taught that God's word comforts, he meant it very broadly, as written in his *Sweet Exposition*:

> **Coverdale:** In the great heat, when the sun doth sore burn (Ps. cxx), and I can have no shade, then he leadeth me to the fresh water, giveth me drink, and refresheth me: that is, in all manner of troubles, anguishes, and necessities, spiritual and bodily, when I know not elsewhere to find help or comfort, I hold me unto the word of grace. There only, and nowhere else, do I find the right consolation and refreshing. (Page 38. Gently updated)

However, from the Geneva Bible onward, rest, repose, and still waters figure most prominently in the new translations of Psalm 23, except for the Roman Catholic Douay-Rheims version:

Psalm 23:1-2 in post-Reformation translations

GNV, 1560/99 The Lord is my shepherd, I shall not want. He maketh me to rest in green pasture, and leadeth me by the still waters.

Bishops' Bible, 1602 God is my shepherd, therefore I can lack nothing. He will cause me to repose myself in pasture full of grass, and he will lead me unto calm waters.

KJV, RV, & JPS (Jewish) The Lord is my shepherd; I shall not want. He maketh me to lie down in green pastures: he leadeth me beside the still waters.

Douay-Rheims, 1899 American Edition The Lord ruleth me: and I shall want nothing. He hath set me in a place of pasture. He hath brought me up, on the water of refreshment.

Orthodox Study Bible, 1982 The Lord is my shepherd; I shall not want. He makes me to lie down in green pastures; He leads me beside the still waters.

NIV, 1984 The Lord is my shepherd, I shall not be in want. He makes me lie down in green pastures, he leads me beside quiet waters.

The Tanakh (Jewish), 1985 The Lord is my shepherd; I lack nothing. He makes me lie down in green pastures; He leads me to waters in places of repose.

Good News Translation, 1992 The Lord is my shepherd; I have everything I need. He lets me rest in fields of green grass and leads me to quiet pools of fresh water.

The Message, 2018 God, my shepherd! I don't need a thing. You have bedded me down in lush meadows, you find me quiet pools to drink from.

ESV, 2020 The Lord is my shepherd; I shall not want. He makes me lie down in green pastures. He leads me beside still waters.

1. PSALM 23: THE WORD OF GOD AS PASTURE AND COMFORT

The post-Reformation translations make it difficult, if not impossible, to relate Psalm 23 to God's word. It is a loss. Furthermore, the emphasis on rest is confusing for believers, many of whom experience much affliction and unrest in their pilgrimage through this life. Paul's assurances to the Thessalonians were not of rest now, but when the Lord Jesus shows himself from heaven (2Th. 1:6-7). Luther wrote, "the Christian life is nothing but a battle and a camp, as Scripture says," and, "even if you are baptized, you must realize that you are never safe from the devil and from sin. Indeed, you must remember that now you will have no peace."[14] He also wrote that the greater a person's faith is, the greater the trials will be.[15] The apostle Paul was moved to complain that "we are killed all day long, and are counted as sheep appointed to be slain" (Ro. 8:36).

Therefore, Scripture does not promise that this life will pass as in a tranquil pasture. Rather, we walk in the valley of the shadow of death, and in this valley the Lord's sheep live by every word that comes from the mouth of God.

> *Christian! Seek not yet repose,*
> *Hear thy guardian angel say;*
> *Thou art in the midst of foes;*
> *Watch and pray!*
>
> *—from the 1836 hymn by*
> *Charlotte Elliott*

---

[14] Martin Luther, "Catholic Epistles," Vol. 30, *Luther's Works*, 71.
[15] Ibid, 70.

2

1 Peter 1:13

The Word Declared to the Soul: Of Faith, Grace, and Hope

> Amazing grace, how sweet the sound
> That saved a wretch like me.
> —*Hymn by John Newton*

IN THIS AND the next chapter, we look at two verses in the New Testament from which valuable and important teaching about the word of God has been taken away through revisions to William Tyndale's translations. These losses have gone completely unnoticed. This may be partly because, as was the case with Psalm 23, the revisions were not made to verses that literally mentioned God's word, but which taught about it through spiritual teaching or imagery.

In the first epistle of the apostle Peter, we enter into the mystery of the revelation of Christ to the human soul through the preaching of the word. This revelation is the unseen giving of him who is the Word, in the power of the Holy Spirit. It brings the grace of divine forgiveness to repentant and believing hearts, makes Christ known to man, and through Christ reconciles man to God. Thus justified by grace in Christ, a man or woman knows God – a gift of infinite and inexpressible value, which is bestowed upon man in the mystery of the Holy Trinity. For as it is written, "We know that the Son of God has come, and has given us a mind to know him who is true. And we are in him who is true through his Son Jesus Christ. This same is very God and eternal life" (1Joh. 5:20).

From Tyndale's translation of 1 Peter 1:13, we learn that this precious gift of grace in Christ Jesus is given by the declaring of Christ; that is, by preaching of him – that he is the Son of God, and that he died for our sins and rose again to life. However, to follow the many revisions to 1 Peter 1:13 in Bibles made after the Reformation Period is to witness the incremental loss of this foundational truth. (It is noteworthy that the new translations that we will see were not due to differences in the underlying Greek manuscripts, but to re-interpretations of the text.)

Tyndale's translation was as follows:

1 Peter 1:13-15, MB [13] Wherefore gird up the loins of your minds, be sober, and *trust perfectly on the grace that is brought unto you by the declaring of Jesus Christ,* [14]as obedient children, not fashioning yourselves unto your old lusts of ignorance: [15]but as he [who] called you is holy, even so be ye holy.

The crucial teaching here is that Christians must trust fully and with a sure confidence on the grace that came to them when Christ was declared to them (and when they believed on him). The verb "declare" means to reveal by speaking forth and instructing in order to make plain and clear. The declaration that brings grace is the plain gospel of Christ and him crucified (1Co. 2:2) – the glad tidings of the New Covenant, which is written in his body and his blood.

In this context, "grace" means the saving grace of God's forgiveness for sin, which delivers a believer from death, hell, and the dominion of Satan. It does not mean the divine influence that governs the administrative gifts or "graces" of believers, which vary from person to person, but the singular grace of forgiveness and gift of justification that is common to all true Christians. This grace comes in the event of salvation when a person hears the declaration of Christ, repents, believes, and is born anew into the life of Christ. (In a different sense, it also comes then in renewal and affirmation when Christ is re-declared and heard again in faith. This is especially so in the service of Holy Communion, where we remember the Passion and work of Christ, and receive of the Testament that is written in his body and his blood.)

The Middle English Wycliffe Bible and the three Reformation Bibles[1] all translated 1 Peter 1:13 according to the understanding that the declaring of Christ brings grace:

1 Peter 1:13

Wycliffe 1380 Hope ye into *the grace that is proffered* to you *by the showing* of Jesus Christ.

COV, MB, GRT Trust perfectly on *the grace that is brought* unto you *by the declaring* of Jesus Christ.

In Wycliffe's 1380 translation, the word "showing" meant declaring or revealing through instruction. This declaration or instruction of Christ is foundational to the going forth of the gospel and ministration of the grace of God for salvation by faith.

Eternal life: The hope and end of salvation, to be shown in the last time

Earlier in the first chapter of 1 Peter, the apostle wrote at verse 3 that faith in Jesus begets the believer "unto a living hope" to enjoy "an inheritance immortal and undefiled." Scripture often

---

[1] Concerning the three Reformation Bibles (Coverdale 1535, the 1537 Matthew Bible, and the Great Bible of 1539-1540), see the Preface, pages 118-119.

speaks of salvation as a way or course that begins with the new birth and ends with this immortal inheritance, which is eternal life:

> **1 Peter 1:3-5, NMB** ³Blessed be God the Father of our Lord Jesus Christ, who through his abundant mercy begat us again unto a living hope by the resurrection of Jesus Christ from death, ⁴to enjoy *an inheritance immortal and undefiled*, and that does not perish, *reserved in heaven* for you, ⁵who are kept by the power of God through faith unto salvation. Which salvation is prepared all ready to be shown in the last time…

Our inheritance, therefore, is eternal life – a life to be lived with glorious new bodies, without sin, in the presence of God. This life will be received after Jesus returns and the general resurrection. In verse 5 above, Peter described the eternal life as the salvation that is "all ready to be shown in the last time." This does not mean that true Christians have not been saved, nor that we have not now received grace. Verse 13 and other verses we will see abundantly testify that we stand now in grace. Peter meant that the immortal life, which is the end of salvation, will at the last be achieved, and will then be fully seen and known for what it is. In the meantime, this life, this salvation, is kept unseen in heaven, and we walk to our heavenly destination sustained by the grace and power of God through faith.

The apostle Paul spoke of eternal life as our hope and promise. To the Colossians he wrote that it is "the hope that is laid up in store for you in heaven" (Col. 1:5). In the epistle to the Hebrews we read of the "promise of eternal inheritance" (Heb. 9:15). All the apostles emphatically held this hope and promise before the new Christian converts. They stressed its importance, and how believers must hold fast to it, and how

2. 1 PETER 1:13: THE WORD DECLARED TO THE SOUL

they must prepare for the life to come by righteous and holy living:

> **2 Peter 1:3 & 5-12, NMB** His divine power has given to us all things that pertain to life and godliness, through the knowledge of him who has called us by virtue and glory, by the means whereof are given to us excellent and most great promises ...
>
> And give all diligence to this. To your faith add virtue, and to virtue knowledge, and to knowledge temperance, and to temperance patience, to patience godliness, to godliness brotherly kindness, to brotherly kindness love. For if these things be among you and abound, they will make you so that you will neither be idle nor unfruitful in the knowledge of our Lord Jesus Christ....
>
> Therefore, brethren, give the more diligence to make your calling and election sure. For if you do such things, you shall never err. Yea, and by this means a grand entering in will be given you into the everlasting kingdom of our Lord and Saviour Jesus Christ. And so I will not be negligent to put you always in mind of such things.

Distinguishing the future hope from the present grace

Though it may truly be said that, once saved and standing in grace, believers have one foot in eternity – for ours is a living hope – still, as we have seen, the Scriptures consistently speak of eternal life as the "promised inheritance" and as "reserved in heaven"; that is, as a *future* thing. For the purpose of the following discussion, it is important to establish that the Scriptures do not speak of grace in the same way, but speak of it as a *present* thing. They do not conflate the present gift of grace with the future inheritance of eternal life as some do (and as will be seen), as if eternal life is the "promised grace" or "grace reserved." Rather, they say that while eternal life is reserved in heaven, grace is given now on earth; grace has appeared, grace has come, we stand in grace now:

Grace is now, NMB

Titus 2:11 The grace of God that brings salvation to all men has appeared.

1 Peter 1:10 Of this salvation have the prophets enquired and searched, who prophesied of the grace that would come to you.

1 Peter 5:12 I have written briefly, exhorting and testifying how this is the true grace of God, wherein you stand.

Romans 5:1-2 We are at peace with God through our Lord Jesus Christ, by whom we have a way in through faith, to this grace wherein we stand and rejoice in the hope of the glory to come, which shall be given by God.

Again, in this context "grace" means the divine mercy by which repentant sinners are reconciled to God through Christ, in the common salvation, with the promise of eternal life:

Titus 3:7-8, NMB He saved us ... by the fountain of the new birth, and with the renewing of the Holy Spirit ... so that we, once justified by his grace, should be heirs of eternal life through hope. This is a true saying.

Therefore, once we are justified and standing in grace, the last gift remaining to us is the eternal life. The apostles always and consistently spoke of Christians as standing in grace now in the hope of this future inheritance. It chanced, while I was writing this, that I was also reading Luther on an unrelated matter, and I noticed how the apostolic doctrine (grace first, then eternal life) undergirded his teaching:

Luther: One must first of all hold fast carefully to this rule, that justification, the forgiveness of sins, grace, or

mercy, come first and are the cornerstone, so to speak....
Thus it is said in Isaiah (65:1): "I was ready to be found by those who did not like me." This should be the cornerstone, and God should be the beginning of our salvation – God, who manifests and reveals himself to us in order that we may learn to know him. This is the principle and the foundation that is set forth in all Scripture.... This is truly the first grace, where we do nothing but are only passive. We hear God speaking the word, and we feel him working through the oral word and the sacraments, through which he awakens us in knowledge of him.... The first gift is the knowledge of God.[2]

Once we possess this precious gift of the knowledge of God by grace, we must hold fast to what we first heard in the declaration of Christ so that we may attain to the eternal life:

1 John 2:24-25, NMB Let therefore abide in you that which you heard from the beginning. If that which you heard from the beginning remains in you, you also will continue in the Son and in the Father. And the promise that he has promised us is eternal life.

Grace deferred is grace lost

But step by step in new Bible translations, through ongoing revisions to Tyndale's translation of 1 Peter 1:13, present grace has become a future gift, and it has become confused with the inheritance of eternal life. It has also become an uncertain gift – something not to be relied on, but only hoped for. This is a significant departure from that which we heard in the beginning,

---

[2] Martin Luther, "Lectures on Genesis," Vol. 5, *Luther's Works*, American Edition (Saint Louis: Concordia Publishing House, 1964), 257-59.

and a manifest failure to hold fast to it. Further, it turns Peter's earnest purpose – to assure the believers that grace received makes their hope sure – on its head.

In the first step of departure, the link between the declaration of Christ and the giving of grace was lost, as we shall see. Once that was lost, present grace was forgotten, and we were diverted from trusting on grace now to hoping for it in the future – even at the second coming, which is the time set for receiving our inheritance. But not only that, the second coming is also the time set for the final judgement. The modern confusion concerning the advent of grace is what Luther might call a fallacy of division and re-composition. The 2011 NIV translation shows just how far this confusion has progressed, and how the departure from Tyndale's original English translation has reached a point of no return in modern Bibles:

1 Peter 1:13, NIV (2011) Set your hope on the grace *to be brought* to you *when* Jesus Christ *is revealed at his coming*.

But, who is a Christian who is not *already* standing in grace? Moreover, who is a Christian to whom Christ has not already been revealed *since* his coming? For "we all behold the glory of the Lord with his face revealed" (2Co. 3:18). But the NIV has corrupted and lost this foundational teaching.

The NIV translation conflates the Christian longing for Jesus' return with the advent of grace, and falsely puts grace at his second coming. One of the pernicious consequences of looking for future grace is that the present gift is overlooked, diminished, neglected, misunderstood. Confidence in grace is then lost, and so also is the hope of our inheritance diminished, because grace has replaced it as our hope. By these means, faith is undermined.

2. 1 PETER 1:13: THE WORD DECLARED TO THE SOUL

Further, the hope for future grace is, properly considered, a false hope, because when Jesus returns it will be too late for grace. He will come then for those who *before believed* (Eph. 1:12); that is, for those who believed before their death, and before his return and the great judgement. For it is appointed to man once to die, and then comes the judgement (Heb. 9:27). The traditional Commination service of the Anglican Church warns concerning the second coming:

> Then shall appear the wrath of God in the day of vengeance, which obstinate sinners, through the stubbornness of their heart, have heaped unto themselves; who despised the goodness, patience, and long sufferance of God, when he calleth them continually to repentance. Then shall they call upon me (saith the Lord) but I will not hear; they shall seek me early, but they shall not find me; and that because they hated knowledge and received not the fear of the Lord, but abhorred my counsel and despised my correction. Then shall it be too late to knock, when the door shall be shut; and too late to cry for mercy, when it is the time of justice. O terrible voice of most just judgment, which shall be pronounced upon them, when it shall be said unto them, Go ye cursed into the fire everlasting, which is prepared for the devil and his angels.
>
> Therefore, brethren, take we heed [in good time], while the day of salvation lasteth. For the night cometh, when none can work. (Canadian Book of Common Prayer, 1918 edition)

When the time for judgement arrives, the time for repentance and grace is past. The Messiah has already come with grace in his hand: "Now, in the end of the world, he has appeared once and for all, to put sin to flight by the offering up of himself" (Heb. 9:26). It is as the Judge that he will return, with vengeance in his hand, to sit upon the seat of his glory, and before him shall be gathered all nations (M't. 25:31-32). Coverdale warned in his *Treatise on Death* that if we die in our sins, without repentance and without grace, we will be lost, and "all repentance and sorrowing from that time forth shall be in vain."[3]

Therefore, the false hope for grace at the second coming of Christ, compounded with the neglect of present grace, is a serious error, because Christ *is now* come, and *today* is the day of grace and salvation (2Co. 6:2).

The importance of the true hope

It is vital to hold fast to the true hope, which, once we are standing in grace, is the hope of eternal life. In Titus 3:8 above, Paul wrote that through it we are made the heirs of eternal life. Elsewhere he wrote that it enlightens the mind to ponder "the riches of his glorious inheritance upon the saints" (Eph. 1:17-19), and that we are saved, or preserved, by the hope of the adoption and deliverance of our bodies to come (Ro. 8:24).

In the epistle to the Hebrews, this hope is described as an anchor of the soul with power to reach into heaven:

> **Hebrews 6:17-19, NMB** God, wanting very much to show to the heirs of promise the certainty of his counsel, added an oath, so that by two immutable things (in which it was impossible that God should lie) we may have perfect consolation – we who have fled to hold fast the hope that is set before us, which hope we have as an anchor of the soul both sure and steadfast. Which hope also enters in, into those things that are within the veil.

---

[3] Myles Coverdale, *Treatise on Death* (Canada: Baruch House Publishing, 2021), 81.

Thus the true Christian hope enters into the things of eternity within the veil. What an amazing hope! The apostle John wrote also that it purifies the soul:

1 John 3:2-3, NMB Dearly beloveds, now we are the children of God. And yet it does not appear what we will be. But we know that when he appears, we shall be like him. For we shall see him as he is. And everyone who has this hope in him purifies himself, even as he is pure.

I believe this purification comes in part because to set our hope on eternal things encourages us to pursue that holiness without which no man will see God (Heb. 12:14). It also liberates us from preoccupation with worldly things, and helps us bear suffering and persecutions patiently. But most of all, it is the way to heaven in truth, and this way must be kept straight and incorrupt.

However, the flesh is weak, and we can barely appreciate the glory of the promised immortality, which we cannot see nor easily conceive of. We cannot believe as we want, nor hope as we ought. Knowing our weakness, the apostles stressed the importance of striving to keep the faith of things unseen, for "we walk in faith, and see not" (2Co. 5:7). And they exhorted the new Christians to confidence and assurance:

Hebrews 3:5-7, NMB And Moses truly was faithful in all his house, as a servant, to bear witness of those things that were to be spoken afterward. But Christ as a son has rule over the house – whose house we are, if so be that we hold fast the confidence and the assurance of that hope to the end.

But the devil also knows our weakness, and endeavours without ceasing to exploit it, and to undermine our faith, confidence, hope, and assurance.

The Geneva Bible revisions and notes

All the Bibles published after the Reformation Period have increasingly employed new nouns, verb tenses, and prepositions to change William Tyndale's translation of 1 Peter 1:13. These revisions have corrupted the message of hope and a sure confidence in present grace.

To begin with, in the Geneva Bible the gerund "declaring" was changed to the noun "revelation." This is workable, but it feeds into the modern error because it enables a visual image more consistent with the future coming of the Lord in the clouds than with the present, unseen revelation of him that comes through the word declared. Happy are those who have not seen and yet believe (Joh. 20:29)!

Nevertheless, it is possible to derive the teaching of present grace from the GNV translation because it retained Tyndale's word "trust" along with the present tense, thus indicating that grace "is brought." (The numbers in brackets below were keyed to the many notes the Puritans added upon this verse.):

> **1 Peter 1:13, GNV 1599** [1]Wherefore [2]gird up the loins of your mind: be sober, [3]and trust [4]perfectly on that grace [5]that *is brought* unto you, [6]*in the revelation* of Jesus Christ.

Standing alone, therefore, the GNV translation allowed the understanding that we receive grace now when Christ is "revealed." It was a poor revision, however, because it obscured the means of revelation (declaration). But worse were the new notes, which introduced the idea that grace is but a future hope. The two pertinent notes are below:

1599 GNV notes on 1 Peter 1:13

Note (3) He setteth forth very briefly, what manner of hope ours ought to be, to wit, continual, until we enjoy

2. 1 PETER 1:13: THE WORD DECLARED TO THE SOUL

> the thing we hope *for*: then, *what we have to hope for, to wit, grace* (that is, free salvation) revealed to us in the Gospel, and not that, that men do rashly and fondly promise to themselves.
>
> **Note (6)** He setteth out the end of faith, lest any man should promise himself, either sooner or later that full salvation, to wit, the later coming of Christ: and therewithal warneth us, not to measure the dignity of the Gospel according to the present state, seeing that that which we are now, is not yet revealed.

The ambiguity and semantic confusion of these notes make it difficult to comment on them, but it is evident that their thrust is to pull the rug out from under a confident trust on present grace. I comment in point form below on only some of the problems I see:

(1) Note 3 leaves the reader wondering just what that rash and fond promise is that men make to themselves, which apparently is the wrong way to salvation. How terrifying! But in no case could it be said that Peter intended to warn the new believers about the unreliability of promises they make to themselves. Not at all. Rather, his purpose was to comfort and strengthen them concerning the promises that are theirs in Christ.

(2) Note 3 also makes grace a future possibility, not a present gift; it destroys the concept of trusting on grace and twists it into a hope. It then conflates that hope with a future "free salvation," as if grace and salvation are not *now* given freely in Christ.

(3) Not only is the doctrine of note 3 false, so are the hermeneutics: it indicates that Peter was exhorting new Christians, who by definition had already received grace, to hope for it.

Contrast Peter and Paul, who exhorted them to stand in it (1Pe. 5:12, Ro. 5:1-2).

(4) Note 6 then undermines confidence in the promise of "full salvation" at the "later coming of Christ": *Don't* promise yourself, it suggests, either sooner or later! Thus, by several devices the GNV notes utterly overthrew Peter's purpose, which was to encourage – not discourage or alarm – the new Christians. How far it was from his purpose to sow seeds of doubt, or to raise a spectre of false promises! No, he wanted to assure the people that they *should* trust on the grace they had received, and on the promises that are theirs *now* in Christ.

(5) The reference in verse 6 to not measuring the *dignity* of the gospel by the present state is a perversion of the concept that we must not measure (to use the GNV term) the *promise* or *hope* of the gospel by the present state. In other words, no matter how hopeless or bleak things might appear, we must cling to God's word and promises. "Dignity" is an irrelevant consideration.

(6) Note 6 says that what we are *now* is not yet revealed, perverting the message that it is *what we will be* that does not yet appear (1Joh. 3:2), or what we will in the future see and know (1Co. 13:12).

Thus did the GNV notes destroy the message that was so clear in Tyndale's translation. And once more (as with the commentaries on Psalm 23), it appears that John Calvin was the source of the new doctrine. However, Calvin's commentary on 1 Peter 1:13 is extraordinarily ambiguous. While he gives a nod to the traditional teaching as expressed in Tyndale's translation, he vacillates between discussions of Christ's past and future comings, and his words can be bent in both directions. Nonetheless, he appears to prefer a future focus, and reinforces the concept of *hoping for* instead of *trusting on* grace – or "graces" as

2. 1 PETER 1:13: THE WORD DECLARED TO THE SOUL

he oddly puts it in places. He also wrote that the Christians must "be prompt to receive grace" when it will be brought to them, again as if they had not received grace, and as if there was something now lacking to them of grace. Further, he suggested, almost as an unbeliever might, that the declaration of Christ is or was a "vain" invitation, although Peter was most certainly writing to those to whom Christ had *not* been declared in vain, and his desire was for them to be confident of that. But Calvin turned the message upside-down:

> **Calvin:** And we must notice the connection: he had said, that so elevated was the kingdom of Christ, to which the gospel calls us, that even angels in heaven desire to see it; what then ought to be done by us who are in the world? *Doubtless, as long as we live on earth, so great is the distance between us and Christ, that in vain he invites us to himself.* It is hence necessary for us to put off the image of Adam and to cast aside the whole world and all hinderances, that being thus set at liberty we may rise upwards to Christ. And he exhorted those to whom he wrote to be prepared and sober, and to *hope for the graces offered* to them, and also to renounce the world and their former life, and to be conformed to the will of God....
>
> Hope to the end, or, perfectly hope. He intimates that *those who let their minds loose on vanity, did not really and sincerely hope for the grace of God*; for though they had some hope, yet as they vacillated and were tossed to and fro in the world, *there was no solidity in their hope*. Then he says, for *the grace which will be brought to you, in order that they might be more prompt to receive it*....
>
> "*At the revelation of Jesus Christ*" *may be explained in two ways*: that the doctrine of the gospel reveals Christ to us; and that, as we see him as yet only through a mirror and enigmatically, *a full revelation is deferred to the last day*. The

first meaning is approved by Erasmus, nor do I reject it. *The second seems, however, to be more suitable to the passage. For the object of Peter was to call us away beyond the world; for this purpose the fittest thing was the recollection of Christ's coming.* For when we direct our eyes to this event, this world becomes crucified to us, and we to the world. Besides, according to this meaning, Peter used the expression shortly before. Nor is it a new thing for the apostles to employ the preposition *en* in the sense of *eis*. Thus, then, I explain the passage, – "You have no need to make a long journey that you may attain the grace of God; for God anticipates you; inasmuch as he brings it to you." But as the fruition of it will not be until Christ appears from heaven, in whom is hid the salvation of the godly, there is need, in the meantime, of hope; for *the grace of Christ is now offered to us in vain, except we patiently wait until the coming of Christ.*[4]

Some observations on this discouraging and ambiguous commentary:

(1) It is not clear which coming of Christ Calvin had in mind when he said, in the third paragraph, that we should "recollect" Christ's coming as in Peter's "expression shortly before," though the context strongly suggests the future coming. Shortly before, in verse 7, Peter had spoken about the future, second coming. Is it the recollection of this future coming that Calvin means would "call us away from this world"? This seems likely, since he speaks of *the world crucified to us*, but never speaks of *Christ crucified for us*, which was the key event of the first coming. However, the world crucified to us has noth-

---

[4] Calvin's commentary on 1 Peter 1:13 is not appended here but may be viewed on any one of numerous online platforms that carry his commentaries.

2. 1 PETER 1:13: THE WORD DECLARED TO THE SOUL

ing to do with 1 Peter 1:13. Also, it is not a "recollection" of the second coming, but the remembrance of Christ crucified in his first coming, which opens the gates of heaven to believers ("Do this, in the remembrance of me…").

(2) Calvin wrote of grace as a future thing in the second paragraph ("grace which will be brought to you,") but contrariwise as a present thing – albeit offered in vain – in the last sentence of the third paragraph above: "the grace of Christ is now offered to us in vain, except we patiently wait until the coming of Christ." Again, how contrary this is to the apostles' reassurance that we stand now in grace received! Furthermore, the third paragraph not only discusses present grace as a thing vainly offered, it makes grace conditional on the second coming. It corrupts the truth that grace is offered in vain when we do not believe that Christ *has come*. Indeed, every spirit that confesses that Jesus Christ has come in the flesh is of God, but every spirit that does not confess that he has come, is an Antichrist (1Jo. 4:2-3, 2Jo. 1:7).

(3) Calvin brought in the unrelated teaching of 1 Corinthians 13:12 concerning the knowledge of God that we will have when we enter into the eternal life. This points us to the future again. Further, here Calvin appears to confuse the divine persons, by asserting that in 1 Corinthians Paul was speaking about a future knowledge of Christ; however, Paul was speaking there more generally of the knowledge of God. (1 Corinthians 13:12 is considered in Part 3 of this Appendix.)

(4) Calvin also said that, apparently despite grace, Christ is at a great distance from us – again, as if he has not come in the flesh, and as if he does not dwell in our hearts by faith (Eph. 3:17); as if the word is not near us now, "even in our mouth and heart" (Ro. 10:6-8); and as if Christ is not now received in grace by declaration – the very teaching of 1 Peter 1:13. But Calvin

taught a faraway, unattainable Christ. "Doubtless," he wrote above, "as long as we live on earth, so great is the distance between us and Christ, that in vain he invites us to himself." In a similar way, as we saw, he taught a faraway God in his commentary on Psalm 23. Thus with many darts he chipped away at a believer's confidence, and also at the doctrine of Christ come in the flesh, while he sowed seeds of doubt and unbelief.

(5) Calvin confused and falsified Peter's teaching about grace when he spoke of it in the plural. In the place of a steadfast trust on grace brought by the declaring of Christ, he wrote that the Christians should "hope for the graces offered to them." This appears to conflate the gifts of grace discussed by Paul in 2 Corinthians 12, which are given to believers to serve the congregation in their various capacities, with the common grace of salvation. Also, by speaking of these graces as "*offered*," he again suggested that the Christians had not received grace(s). Indeed, if that was true, then their hope really was vain, as Calvin spoke of it.

All is confusion in Calvin's doctrine, all is subtly false, all is discouraging. With appearances of erudition and righteousness he in effect taught another gospel – a gospel with uncertain ladders and uncertain graces, with a distant saviour who is not Emmanuel, God with us, and with no confident trust; that is, no real faith. Who but an Antichrist would so distort Peter's purpose and message?

The future focus in the KJV translation

In the 1611 King James Bible, further revisions to Tyndale's translation pointed the reader even more definitely to the future for grace:

1 Peter 1:13, KJV Hope to the end for the grace that *is to be brought* unto you *at the revelation* of Jesus Christ.

2. 1 PETER 1:13: THE WORD DECLARED TO THE SOUL

These changes took us several steps closer to the modern translations. First, the KJV changed "trust" to "hope," a clear future focus in accordance with Calvin and the GNV notes. Perhaps the Calvinist influence also prompted the change of tense to the future perfect ("*is to be* brought"). Finally, the KJV introduced the preposition "at," which denotes placement in time (*at* the revelation) instead of instrumentality (*by* preaching). The loss of the original meaning was nearly complete with these changes, as Geneva's future hope moved from expository notes into the translation itself.

It might be argued that the KJV rendering still allows for the concept that grace is now brought *at* the revelation of Jesus Christ through preaching. However, again the hermeneutics are wrong, because Peter was writing to believers who had already received grace, and to whom Christ had already been revealed. It is incongruous to exhort them to hope for that which they had already received.

The new preposition "at" in the KJV did not only lose the concept of the instrumentality of the word to declare Christ to the soul, but, taken with the new future tense, it prepared the way for pre-millennialism. Millenarian doctrines come in many forms and permutations, but the thread that unites them all is the idea that, after this present age or season, there will be a future period of grace connected with a future reign of the saints or of Christ on earth. Such doctrine undermines the understanding that now is the kingdom of grace, and that Christ reigns now in the hearts and consciences of his people. For the fulfilment of the ages is now upon us: behold, now is that well-favoured time; behold, now is that day of salvation (2Co. 6:2). John the Baptist cried out to the people of the first century to repent and believe, for the kingdom of heaven was then at hand.

Thomas Cranmer, who drafted the Articles of Religion for the Church of England, condemned millenarianism in an early Article, where he described it as a "fable of heretics" and Jewish error.[5] Clearly, millenarian teaching derogates from the glory of Christ's present kingdom. And again, concerning the divine grace, the gospel calls us to look *back* in time, in remembrance of Christ's first coming and the events thereof.[6] One purpose of the Lord's Supper, the sacrament of the body and blood of the Lord, is to quicken this reflection. Peter counted it of vital importance to put the Christians in remembrance of the first coming and all that it entails:

> **2 Peter 1:15-16, NMB** I will do my best to ensure, therefore, that on every side you have something with which to stir up the remembrance of these things after my departing. For we were not following deceitful fables when we made known to you the power and coming of our Lord Jesus Christ…

If we turn our hope away from him who has already come with grace in his hands to another hope, or to another time, we are no longer trusting perfectly on grace received, as Peter urged.

Modern Bibles and the hope for future grace

In modern Bibles, the doctrine of grace received by the declaration of Christ has been lost beyond recovery. See what has hap-

---

[5] Former Article 41 of Cranmer's Articles of Religion read, "HERETICS CALLED MILLENARII: They that go about to renew the fable of heretics, called Millenarii, be repugnant to Holy Scripture, and cast themselves headlong into a Jewish dotage." Unfortunately, this Article was removed in 1563.

[6] Myles Coverdale wrote eloquently about this in *Fruitful Lessons upon the Passion, Burial, Resurrection, Ascension, and of the Sending of the Holy Ghost*, published by Baruch House in 2021 as part of this Coverdale Books series.

pened to the preposition "by" over time. After morphing to "in" (1599 GNV) and then "at" (KJV), it is not even a preposition any more in some of the modern versions, but has become "when," a conjunction of time used with reference to the second coming:

1 Peter 1:13 in the Modern Period

RV Set your hope perfectly on the grace that **is to be brought* unto you *at the revelation of Jesus Christ*. (**RV note:** **Gr. is being brought.*)

RSV Set your hope fully upon the grace that *is coming* to you *at the revelation of Jesus Christ*.

JB Put your trust in nothing but the grace that *will be given* you *when Jesus Christ is revealed*.

LB So now you can *look forward* soberly and intelligently to more of God's kindness to you *when Jesus Christ returns*.

NKJV Rest your hope fully upon the grace that *is to be brought* to you *at the revelation of Jesus Christ*.

NIV 1984 Set your hope fully on the grace *to be given* you *when Jesus Christ is revealed*.

NIV 2011 Set your hope on the grace to be brought to you when Jesus Christ is revealed at his coming.

ESV Set your hope fully on the grace that will be brought to you at the revelation of Jesus Christ.

In the modern Bibles, not only must we look to the future for grace, in the Living Bible it is not even grace any more. The RV note above is interesting. It shows the literal translation of the Greek verb in the present progressive ("*is being* brought"). In standard English, this would be rendered as Tyndale had it: "*is* brought."

The New Matthew Bible alone among modern versions guarded Tyndale's meaning intact and uncorrupt:

> **1 Peter 1:13-23, NMB** Therefore gird up the loins of your minds, be sober, and trust fully on the grace that is brought to you by the declaring of Jesus Christ, as obedient children – not fashioning yourselves to your old lusts of ignorance, but as he who called you is holy, you also be holy, in all manner of conduct, because it is written: Be holy, for I am holy.

Final thoughts

Modern commentators do not completely deny present grace; however, they shake the foundations of the faith by speaking of a mere beginning of grace now, as in the popular Zondervan commentary below. (This commentary also undermines Paul's teaching in 2 Corinthians 3:18 that believers now see Christ with his face unveiled, the spiritual "seeing" of the present salvation):

> **NIV Zondervan commentary (1994):** The main emphasis of v.13 is on putting one's hope wholly in the final consummation of the grace of God in Jesus Christ. At the present time, we enjoy only a beginning of that grace (cf 1Jn 3:2-3). This longing for the unveiling of Jesus at his second coming permeates the NT.

Certain verses in modern Bibles have been rewritten to expressly refer to a future "consummation" of grace. That the future will see a consummation of *hope* is true, and that this comes of grace is true, but still this does not teach grace and hope as the apostles did: we stand in grace now in the hope of eternal life.

Martin Luther always wrote and taught not to discourage believers, as Calvin and the Geneva notes did, but, rather, to build trust, confidence, and hope – especially when things seem

2. 1 PETER 1:13: THE WORD DECLARED TO THE SOUL

most hopeless. In his lectures on Genesis, he held up the patriarch Jacob as an example for us, even today. Jacob had received a divine blessing from Isaac, but was then sent into exile and terribly difficult circumstances for twenty years, where everything seemed contrary to the promises that he had received. This is an example for us, who, after receiving divine grace, live by faith as strangers in exile in this world, and often in suffering, while we await the promises. Luther did not teach a vain invitation in Christ like Calvin did, nor a faraway saviour, but he urged and wrote:

> [W]hat is begun through faith is not yet in one's possession but is hoped for. Thus God has promised us eternal life, and has given absolution and baptism. This grace I have at hand through Christ, but I await eternal life, which is promised in the word.... And let us wait for the promise itself in hope and longsuffering, for God will not lie.[7]

---

[7] Luther, "Lectures on Genesis," *Luther's Works,* Vol. 5, 183.

3

1 Corinthians 13:12
The Sight of the Word

> Meanwhile, we have the light in a mystery.
> —*Martin Luther*

IF THE GRACE OF FORGIVENESS is now full in Christ Jesus our Lord, our knowledge of God is not full – not as long as we are in the flesh.

In 1 Corinthians 13, the apostle Paul wrote about our present, imperfect knowledge of God and of divine things. Our knowledge comes by the word of God: by his written or spoken word, and thus, mysteriously but really, by the Son who is the Word. First comes faith by hearing, and in hearing and believing we receive the Son by the Holy Spirit, who reveals God to us in the Holy Trinity. Thus by the word we may know God, and may learn about him. However, our knowledge will remain imperfect until we enter the eternal life – at which time, Paul assured the Corinthians, we will know as fully as we are known.

In William Tyndale's translation of 1 Corinthians 13:12, the word of God was depicted figuratively as a "glass" in which we see, and was also described as a "dark speaking." These metaphors are difficult to understand today, due to changes in English semantics over the centuries. In 1535, Tyndale translated:

1 Corinthians 13:9-12, MB ⁹For our knowledge is unperfect, and our prophesying is unperfect. ¹⁰But when that which is perfect is come, then that which is unperfect shall be done away. ¹¹When I was a child, I spoke as a child, I understood as a child, I imagined as a child. But as soon as I was a man, I put away childishness. ¹²*Now we see in a glass, even in a dark speaking*, but then shall we see face to face. Now I know unperfectly, but then shall I know even as I am known.

In verse 12, the word "even" is epexegetical; that is, it indicates that the following words ("in a dark speaking") add information about what went before ("in a glass"). Today we might say, "Now we see in a glass; namely, in a dark speaking." Therefore, the "glass" in which we see and the "dark speaking" are one and the same thing. But what is that thing? It is the word of God. However, the old imagery is very obscure.

Tyndale's word "glass" is both archaic and ambiguous. Some say it means a "perspective glass," which is an old name for a monocle, magnifying glass, or other lens that assists vision. However, it may also have meant "mirror" in an obsolete sense. Wycliffe used "mirror" in verse 12 in his 1380 English Bible. His translation was, "We see now by a mirror in darkness." However, then the word "mirror" meant something different than it does today; it referred figuratively to anything that gave a true description of something else.[1] In modern Eng-

---

[1] OED online, s.v. "mirror," entry I.3.a. "Mirror: A thing regarded as giving a true description of something else." Another example from Wycliff is, "[Wisdom] is..a merour with oute wem of þe maieste of god." The word "mirror" is sometimes used in this sense today, but only in limited contexts. With reference to persons, as Wycliffe used it (OED entry I.3.b), it was obsolete by the 18th century. Another obsolete figurative use of "mirror" was to indicate a model of excellence (entry I.1.b).

lish idiom, we could say that the word *reflects* God to us; however, to describe it as a mirror no longer conveys the correct idea, because we understand a mirror to be a sheet of reflective glass in which we see *ourselves*; our own image is reflected back to us. We do not understand "mirror" in the obsolete figurative sense, as a thing that reflects the image of something or someone that is absent, in the way that the word reflects God.

Therefore, Paul used the imagery of a lens or mirror metaphorically to teach that God's word reveals or reflects God to us, but the metaphor does not serve well in modern English.

"Dark speaking" in verse 12 is a noun phrase that translates the Greek noun *ainigma* ("enigma"), which refers to mysterious words or speech. In older English, and also in German, the adjective "dark" was used to describe speech that is difficult to understand.[2] In his 1534 New Testament, Martin Luther translated verse 12 so as to make it clear that God's word is this "dark speaking" or enigma:

1 Corinthians 13:12, Luther 1534 Wir sehen jizt durch einen Spiegel *inn einem tuncteln wort.* (Original spelling)

In English, this is "We see now through a glass *in a dark word.*"[3] Thus our "sight" of God and of spiritual things comes by this

---

Thus, it was a word pregnant with meaning for readers in centuries past, but the meaning is lost to us now.

[2] OED online s.v. "dark," adjective, entry 6.a. A quotation from 1687: "He's a little dark in this paragraph; but the change of one word will make him ... clear."

[3] I make the updated German to be, *"Wir sehen jetzt durch einen Spiegel in einem dunklen Wort."* *Spiegel* might be translated "mirror" also, but as Luther expounds this verse, it does not reflect his meaning. He often spoke of spiritual seeing as with a light shining *through* the word, or through faith, through the sacrament, or through the humanity of Christ (e.g. *Luther's Works,* American Edition, Vol. 11 at p. 548 and Vol. 52 at p. 72). Light does not shine "through" mirrors but is reflected from them. However, perhaps "Spiegel" was also used in the same figurative sense that "mirror" was formerly in English. I have not investigated this question.

dark, this mysterious, this deep word. The sight it gives is personal, spiritual, and experiential knowledge of the divine, but for now our knowledge is imperfect.

New translations shift the emphasis and change the message

Tyndale and Luther kept close to the original text by putting a noun phrase for the Greek noun (dark speaking/*tuncteln wort* = *enigma*). This more literal rendering guarded the foundational concept. However, beginning again with the Geneva Bible, revisions to the original translation have increasingly obscured it. (And again, the new translations that we will see were not due to variations in the Greek text, but to the revisers' interpretation of it.) In the Geneva Bible, the revisers began by changing the parts of speech:

1 Corinthians 13:12, GNV 1560 & 1599 For now we see *through a glass darkly*: but then shall we see face to face.

The GNV changed the phrasing from "in + noun phrase" ("in a dark speaking") to "through + noun + adverb" ("through a glass darkly"). Of course, it is not wrong for a translator to use different parts of speech if necessary to convey the intended message accurately. However, in this case the revision wrongly emphasized a *manner of* seeing (darkly or poorly) instead of *the thing in or by which* we see (the dark speaking; the word). This re-emphasis subtly distorted the foundational concept, that it is in or by the word that we see. Thus God's word was no longer the main point, but our "dark" sight or seeing.

Moreover, a note on verse 12, new in the 1599 edition of the Geneva Bible, added two more twists to the message. These twists almost imperceptibly hinted that people – that is, the lay people – *may not* know or learn about God from his word. First the note referred the *enigma*, not to the word in itself, but to the "tongues," which was a reference to the Hebrew and Greek

3. 1 CORINTHIANS 13:12: THE SIGHT OF THE WORD

tongues. It taught that "light" – which could only, in the context, refer to the light of spiritual seeing – is given "through the understanding of tongues" – that is, of Hebrew and Greek.

God's word is God's word no matter what language it is in, but, as will be seen, the GNV note subtly suggested that the word in translation – that is, in our own languages of English, German, Spanish, etc. – is somehow not adequate to know God. What then are we to do if we do not know the tongues? Where do we go for "light"? This leads to the next twist: the idea that we must learn about God from the clerics and ministers of the Church, because they are the ones who (so we are to believe) understand the tongues. As we have seen, the Geneva Puritans claimed that their understanding of the tongues was superior to that of the previous English translators.[4] They, therefore, were the ministers from whom the laity must learn about God and heavenly things.

The long GNV note begins:

GNV 1599 note on 1 Corinthians 13:12: The applying of the similitude of our childhood to this present life, wherein we darkly behold heavenly things, according to the small measure of light which is given us through the understanding of tongues, and hearing the teachers and ministers of the Church [etc.].

Therefore, to learn about heavenly things the people must rely on their ministers – to, ironically, receive their "small measure of light" – because they understand the tongues.

Also ironically, though very subtly, this doctrine is a step back to the Roman Catholic position. Rome turned the people to the ministers (and ceremonies) of the church for divine in-

---

[4] See note 4 in the Preface to this Appendix.

struction while denying them vernacular Bible translations. Who but Antichrist would deny people the word of God in their own language? But the GNV commentators, by saying the people should hear ministers who understand the tongues, and at the same time tacitly discounting vernacular translations, hinted covertly at what the Roman Catholic Church asserted openly; the people had the word in their own language, but it was not sufficient, because they lacked understanding of the tongues. The result was to turn the people to their ministers again (and to their sermons) as the fount of the knowledge of God.

The Puritans did not, of course, deny the people an English Bible. But first they changed the Bible, as Tyndale and Coverdale had given it to us, and then they tacitly, in their note, denied that it could or should stand alone. They did this even after claiming to have corrected the original translations.[5] But they also, as they acknowledged in their Bible preface, made the Scriptures more difficult ("hard") to understand.[6] All this meant that God's word required their exposition, and it served to draw the people back into captivity to the Church. A harder translation also meant that some of the meaning was robbed.

The struggle for vernacular Bibles was one of the major battles of the Reformation. Men fought and died to give God's word to the people in their own languages, so that they could have and understand the Scripture for themselves – even, as Tyndale famously said, so the ploughboy could understand it better than the clerics of the Church. The ploughboy needs the word in his own language precisely so that he is not obliged to

---

[5] Ibid. They claimed they "perused and reformed" Tyndale and Coverdale's work.
[6] See the Preface to this Appendix, note 5.

3. 1 CORINTHIANS 13:12: THE SIGHT OF THE WORD

rely on the clerics, who only too often reveal that they indeed possess little light, despite their Greek and Hebrew studies. For no matter how well they understand the tongues, it avails them nothing if they do not have minds renewed by the Holy Spirit to understand spiritual things (1Co. 2:14). Indeed, God chose fishermen and publicans to be his chief ambassadors, not the doctors of the law, the learned, or the wise. Because of the risk of false teaching from the doctors, Tyndale wrote that we need a "meteyard," or measuring stick, to test and judge their doctrine. That meteyard is the word of God plainly and truly translated into vernacular languages, and to provide the people with such a meteyard was a foremost goal of the true Reformers.

Yet another irony in the web of ironies knit into the 1599 GNV note is that it was written by teachers and ministers who claimed to have corrected Tyndale and Coverdale's translations with the superior "clear light" that God had revealed uniquely to them.[7] However, with this note they suggested their translation was not clear enough to test their light[8] – and, therefore, their preaching and teaching must be the final authority for the knowledge of God and his word. So much for the ploughboy's meteyard.

Calvin's commentary on 1 Corinthians 13 does not appear to have been the source of the new doctrine in the 1599 GNV note. He acknowledged that the word of God was the "glass" of verse 12, and he did not refer it to the tongues. However, he

---

[7] Ibid, note 4.
[8] As mentioned, the preface to the Geneva Bible acknowledged that the Puritan treatment of Hebrew idioms made the Scriptures "hard" to understand (see note 6 above). So great has been the Geneva influence, many moderns expect to consult Hebrew or Greek linguistic resources to be able to understand the Bible properly. This effectively turns every reader into his own translator.

introduced more confusion. He wrote that the dark speaking has "nothing ... dark" in it, but then swerved and said it is "comparatively obscure." Then he doubled back again and argued for its clarity, even suggesting that it is wicked to expect greater revelation of God than we now have through his word. He wrote, "For we have in the word (in so far as is expedient for us) a naked and open revelation of God, and it has nothing intricate in it, to hold us in suspense, as wicked persons imagine."[9]

However, it is certainly not wicked to be in an attitude of waiting, and to hope for a more open revelation of God – that is, to expect to know him in the future better than we know him now. That better knowing will happen when we enter into the eternal life. This was Paul's very promise: "Now I know imperfectly, but then I shall know even as I am known." But Calvin effectively contradicted the apostle here, though he, superficially at least, affirmed Paul's teaching in his commentary on 1 Peter 1:13, as we saw in Part 2.[10]

The history of translations of 1 Corinthians 13:12

Following are some translations of 1 Corinthians 13:12 from Wycliffe to today. As mentioned, the words "glass" and "mirror" are confusing due to the different meanings they have in modern English:

1 Corinthians 13:12

Wycliffe 1380 We see now *by a mirror in darkness*: but then face to face.

---

[9] These quotations from John Calvin's commentary at biblehub.com. Accessed July 6, 2021.
[10] See page 169.

3. 1 CORINTHIANS 13:12: THE SIGHT OF THE WORD

COV Now we see *through a glass in a dark speaking*: but then shall we see face to face.

MB, GRT Now we see *in a glass, even in a dark speaking*: but then shall we see face to face.

GNV 1599 For now we see *through a glass darkly*: but then shall we see face to face.

KJV For now we see *through a glass, darkly*; but then face to face.

RV For now we see *in a mirror, *darkly*; but then face to face. (**RV note:** Gr. *in a riddle*)

JB Now we are seeing *a dim reflection in a mirror*; but then we shall be seeing face to face.

NIV 1973 Now we see *but a poor reflection*; then we shall see face to face.

NIV 2011 For now we see *only a reflection as in a mirror*; then we shall see face to face.

ESV For now we see *in a mirror dimly*, but then face to face.

Here the RV note shows that the Greek literally indicated *the thing* in or through which we see God, as Wycliffe, Coverdale, and Tyndale had it, rather than *how* we see, as in the Geneva and KJV revisions.

Certain of the modern Bibles did well to return to the substantive-for-substantive construction, but again, the concept of seeing God in a "mirror," as we now understand this word, is confusing. Some modern commentators, possibly not understanding the old meanings of "mirror," say the ancients used this word because in their time mirrors gave a poor reflection, as if Paul meant to say that God's word is a poor reflection of the divine. This perhaps reveals how the GNV emphasis on seeing "darkly" has unconsciously influenced them. However, in my view Paul could only have meant that God's word is a *true*, albeit mysterious, reflection of the divine. Thus the word reveals or reflects God *to* us *truly*, not *back to* us *poorly*, as the modern semantics of "mirror" suggest.

The earliest editions of the New Matthew Bible retained Tyndale's translation, "Now we see in a glass, even in a dark speaking." However, after comments that this was too obscure, in 2022 it was updated, partly guided by Wycliffe and Luther, to:

> **NMB (October Testament)** Now we see as is reflected to us in a mysterious word, but then we shall see face to face.

It is important to properly convey Paul's message about the place and importance of God's word for Christian "sight." And by this mysterious word all faithful people, be they ploughboy, maiden, or minister, may in this life find the knowledge of the truth and of him who is the truth, with a perfect knowledge to be attained in the next.

> *Haste then on from grace to glory,*
> *Armed by faith and winged by prayer;*
> *Heaven's eternal day's before thee,*
> *God's own hand shall guide thee there.*
>
> *Soon shall close thy earthly mission,*
> *Swift shall pass thy pilgrim days;*
> *Hope soon change to glad fruition,*
> *Faith to sight, and prayer to praise.*
>
> —from the 1824 hymn by Rev. H. F. Lyte

4

Keeping unto the Word

*Corruptions and distortions of the word are a horrible wrath of God ...
For if you do not want to listen to God in his sure truth,
then indeed you may listen to falsehood under the guise of truth,
as Paul in 2 Thessalonians 2:10-11 declares.*
—*Martin Luther*

THE LOST TEACHINGS about God's word – teachings that were knowingly altered or taken away through the Bible revisions and new commentaries that we have seen – are significant. Perhaps of most concern are the revisions to 1 Peter 1:13, which corrupted the excellent knowledge of the grace that is brought through the declaration of Christ. With the new future focus, certain grace has been reduced to an uncertain hope and conflated with the second coming. This undermines the true knowledge of Christ's first coming in the flesh with grace in his hand, the holy remembrance of the cross, confidence in the promises, and the hope of eternal life.

The promises for those who believe

It is fitting to close with a few of the chief lessons from the *Sweet Exposition on Psalm 23*, so that readers may be left with encouragement and strengthening of faith. I have gently updated the passages below for clarity so that their blessing may be full; they are worthy to be read and reread. The numbers in brackets are the pages of this volume where the original passage is given.

The fruits of the word (pp. 37-38)

As for the people of God, or the holy congregation of Christ, the prophet calls it a green meadow. For it is a pleasant garden, adorned and beautified with all manner of spiritual gifts. The pasture or grass therein is the word of God, whereby consciences are strengthened and refreshed....

This is now the first fruit of the word of God: that the Christians are so instructed thereby that they increase in faith and hope, learn to commit all their doings to God, and whatever they have need of, either in soul or body, they look for it at his hand....

This is the second fruit of God's word: it is to the faithful not only pasture and grass, by which they are filled and strengthened in faith, but it is also to them a goodly, cold, fresh water, whereby they take refreshing, comfort, and encouragement.

The word the true riches (pp. 38-39)

This lesson should we learn also; namely, to let the world boast of their great riches, honour, power, etc. For these are insecure, uncertain, and transitory wares, which God casts into the dungeon. It is a small matter for him to give an ungracious person who blasphemes and dishonours him, for his reward, a kingdom, a dukedom, or any other benefit and good upon the earth. These worldly goods are his draff and swillings, with which he fills the hogs' bellies, whom he is disposed to kill.

But to his children, as David says here, he gives the right treasure. Therefore we should not, as the dear children and heirs of God, boast about our wisdom, strength, or riches, but of this: that we have the precious pearl, even that worthy word, whereby we know God our loving father and Jesus Christ whom he has sent. This is our treasure and inheritance, which is sure and everlasting, and better than all the goods of the world.

The word keeps us in the right way so that we are not deceived by false teachers, who know how to pretend holiness (pp. 40-41)

[David says,] the Lord my faithful shepherd does not only feed me in a green meadow and lead me to the fresh water, and so quicken my soul, but he brings me forth also in the right way so that I do not go aside, go astray, and so perish. That is, he holds me fast to the pure doctrine, so that I am not deceived by false spirits, and so that I do not fall away by any other temptation or offence; for example, so that I may know how I should conduct myself outwardly and lead my life, and so that I do not allow myself to be persuaded by the holiness and asceticism of hypocrites; and again, so that I may know what is the true doctrine, faith, and service of God, etc....

For the devil also can pretend holiness and transform himself into an angel of light, as Saint Paul says. Even so likewise, his ministers can show themselves as if they were the preachers of righteousness, and come in sheep's clothing among the flock of Christ, but inwardly they are ravening wolves. Therefore it is good to watch and pray, as the prophet does in the last verse, that our shepherd may keep us by this treasure that he has given us.

However, if God's word has been altered, it is more difficult for the sheep to discern departures from the right way. Alterations have, unfortunately, been sown in many places in the Bible, in both the Old and New Testaments; what we have seen here is but the tip of the iceberg. Many verses in the modern Bibles would be unrecognizable to 16th century readers.

Coverdale stressed that if we want to hold fast to the treasure of the word, we must learn the Shepherd's voice:

Keep thee unto the word (p. 31)

You can do nothing except apply your ears to hear, and with thanksgiving to receive, such an inexpressible treasure, and to learn to know well the voice of the shepherd, to follow him, and to eschew the voice of strangers. Therefore, if you wish to be richly provided for both in body and soul, above all things take good heed then to the voice of the shepherd. Hearken well to what he says to you. Let him feed you, rule you, guide you, defend you, comfort you, etc. That is to say, keep thee unto his word. Be glad to hear it and to learn it, and so no doubt will you be well provided for, both in body and soul.

To understand and keep ourselves unto the word, we do not need to know Greek or Hebrew, as suggested in the GNV note on 1 Corinthians 13:12. Such learning did not assist the scholars who changed the verses we have seen to keep themselves unto the word, nor did it enable them to guide us to it. Quite the opposite; they took the word away. Nor do we need to know Greek or Hebrew to judge the merit or demerit of their new translations. We need a spiritual mind, through faith and the new birth (1Co. 2:14), and a mind informed by trustworthy translations and teaching.

The Scriptures prove these things to be true. The scribes and Pharisees knew Hebrew as well as anyone. They kept the Hebrew scrolls in their synagogues and read and expounded them every Sabbath. The Old Testament prophecies of the Messiah were of especial concern and interest to them, but when their Messiah came, they crucified him. They also chased the true believers out of their congregations (Joh. 9:34), as do the scribes and Pharisees of every generation. For all their great learning, they shut up the kingdom of God before men (M't. 23:13) – as do also the scribes and Pharisees of every generation. For a sound understanding does not belong to the wise, but to the little flock that believes on Christ (1Co. 1:27). Neither does it depend on what languages we know, but on faith, and on truly knowing Christ by the new birth (Joh. 3:3, Gal. 6:15) – and on having the true word of God, even in our own tongue.

Further, it is noteworthy that the knowledge of tongues that the Holy Spirit gave to the apostles and early disciples was the ability to speak *vernacular* languages. They received this miraculous gift so that they could preach the message of Christ to all people in all nations in their own tongues – for it is the message that matters, and not the tongue, except insofar as it is the vehicle for the message. The message remains the same, whatever the tongue. In the miracle of Pentecost the people heard the disciples speaking in their own language and prophesying, speaking of the great works of God. The apostle Luke described this event:

> And there were dwelling at Jerusalem Jews, devout men, who were from all nations under heaven. Hearing of this, a large crowd came together. And the people were astonished because everyone heard them speak his own tongue. They all wondered and marveled, saying among themselves, Are not all these who speak from Galilee? And how is that we hear each his own tongue in which he was born? Parthians, Medes, and Elamites, and the inhabiters of Mesopotamia, of Judea, and of Cappadocia, of Pontus and Asia, Phrygia, Pamphylia, and of Egypt, and of the parts of Libya adjoining Cyrene, and strangers from Rome, Jews and converts, Greeks and Arabians: we have heard them speak with our own tongues about the great

works of God. They were all amazed, and wondered, saying to one another, What does this mean? (Acts 2:5-12)

After this miracle, Peter, empowered by the Holy Spirit, as Coverdale wrote in the *Sweet Exposition*, "smote about him with his sword"; that is, he opened his mouth and preached the word of God, and felled down three thousand souls at once from the power of the devil" (p. 54).

It was the plain, full, true declaration of Christ heard in their own languages, and that alone, which brought grace, salvation, and the light of the knowledge of God. And again, a major issue of the Reformation, and also of John Wycliffe's battle for the Scriptures in his time, was the principle that the word of God, with its promises of eternal life and the forgiveness of sins in Christ Jesus, should – and can, in all fruitfulness and blessedfulness – be given to people in their own languages.

What the sheep need, therefore, is a true translation of God's word in their own tongue. And the best pasture for the sheep is in the original, blood-bought translations of the true Reformers, men who knew the Shepherd and his word, and who knew how to wield the spiritual sword he had given into their hands. Wycliffe's Middle English version, Luther's German Bible, and the three English Reformation Bibles were the works of such men. God called and equipped them, against all the roaring of Antichrist, to furnish the table of the saints richly, for them to eat and drink thereof – "For," Coverdale wrote, "to eat and drink is called in the Scripture, to believe, to take sure hold on God's word, from which follows peace, joy, comfort, strength, etc." When the table is well set with a true knowledge and understanding, then are the sheep nourished and strengthened, so that they may say, when put down and afflicted in the world, surrounded by enemies, and even threatened with death, "The Lord is my shepherd, I can want nothing."

4. KEEPING UNTO THE WORD

FROM THIS REVIEW of three important biblical passages which, in the Reformation Bibles, taught about the place, ministry, and great worth of the word of God, it is evident that with the advent of the Geneva version and the influence of John Calvin, these teachings were put down. The true place of the word, as the foundation of all that matters, was usurped by new translations and expositions. The esteem in which the Reformers Martin Luther, Myles Coverdale, William Tyndale, and John Rogers held the word was forgotten, and a true reverence for the ministry and promises of the word suffered subtly but significantly under the treatment of Calvin and the Geneva Puritans. It is also clear that we may not consider Calvin, nor those who subscribed to his teaching and doctrine, as fellow Reformers with Luther, Coverdale, Tyndale, and Rogers. We have seen enough to know that they spoke with different spirits. Further, when men depart in this much, they will depart in much more.

God's word is life. It raises us up by him who is the Word, so that by his Spirit we may live in his resurrection life. And God's word is truth; by it we are taught and kept in the right way. But without the word there is no life, no truth, no salvation. Satan, who is God's implacable enemy and the enemy of man, life, truth, and all that is good, labours without ceasing to rob us of the word and the fullness of the truth of the word. If force does not avail, still there are a thousand subtle devices, and false appearances of righteousness and scholarly erudition, by which he turns the word to vanity and lies, and so draws the unsuspecting into increasing darkness. Therefore, Coverdale urged, "Keep thee unto the word."

Schedule A

John Calvin's Commentary on Psalm 23

This document is in the public domain and available on websites that offer Bible commentaries. This is the full commentary, unamended except to subdivide it into numbered paragraphs for ease of reference. Notes follow at the end.

Verse 1

1.1 Jehovah is my shepherd. Although God, by his benefits, gently allures us to himself, as it were by a taste of his fatherly sweetness, yet there is nothing into which we more easily fall than into a forgetfulness of him, when we are in the enjoyment of peace and comfort. Yea, prosperity not only so intoxicates many, as to carry them beyond all bounds in their mirth, but it also engenders insolence, which makes them proudly rise up and break forth against God. Accordingly, there is scarcely a hundredth part of those who enjoy in abundance the good things of God, who keep themselves in his fear, and live in the exercise of humility and temperance, which would be so becoming.

1.2 For this reason, we ought the more carefully to mark the example which is here set before us by David, who, elevated to the dignity of sovereign power, surrounded with the splendor of riches and honours, possessed of the greatest abundance of temporal good things, and in the midst of princely pleasures, not only testifies that he is mindful of God, but calling to remembrance the benefits which God had conferred upon him, makes them ladders by which he may ascend nearer to Him.

1.3 By this means he not only bridles the wantonness of his flesh, but also excites himself with the greater earnestness to gratitude, and the other exercises of godliness, as appears from the concluding sentence of the psalm, where he says, "I shall dwell in the house of Jehovah for a length of days." In like manner, in the 18 psalm, which was composed at a period of his life when he was applauded on every side, by calling himself the servant of God, he showed the humility and simplicity of heart to which he had attained, and, at the same time, openly testified his gratitude, by applying himself to the celebration of the praises of God.

1.4 Under the similitude of a shepherd, he commends the care which God, in his providence, had exercised towards him. His language implies that God had no less care of him than a shepherd has of the sheep who are committed to his charge. God, in the Scripture, frequently takes to himself the name, and puts on the character of a shepherd, and this is no mean token of his tender love towards us. As this is a lowly and homely manner of speaking, He who does not disdain to stoop so low for our sake, must bear a singularly strong affection towards us.

1.5 It is therefore wonderful, that when he invites us to himself with such gentleness and familiarity, we are not drawn or allured to him, that we may rest in safety and peace under his guardianship. But it should be observed, that God is a shepherd only to those who, touched with a sense of their own weakness and poverty, feel their need of his protection, and who willingly abide in his sheepfold, and surrender themselves to be governed by him. David, who excelled both in power and riches, nevertheless frankly confessed himself to be a poor sheep, that he might have God for his shepherd.

1.6 Who is there, then, amongst us, who would exempt himself from this necessity, seeing our own weakness sufficiently shows that we are more than miserable if we do not live under the protection of this shepherd? We ought to bear in mind, that our happiness consists in this, that his hand is stretched forth to govern us, that we live under his shadow, and that his providence keeps watch and ward over our welfare. Although, therefore, we have abundance of all temporal good things, yet let us be assured that we cannot be truly happy unless God vouchsafe to reckon us among the number of his flock. Besides, we then only attribute to God the office of a Shepherd with due and rightful honour, when we are persuaded that his providence alone is sufficient to supply all our necessities. As those who enjoy the greatest abundance of outward good things are empty and famished if God is not their shepherd; so it is beyond all doubt that those whom he has taken under his charge shall not want a full abundance of all good things. David, therefore, declares that he is not afraid of wanting any thing, because God is his Shepherd.

Verse 2

2.1 He maketh me to lie down in pastures of grass. With respect to the words, it is in the Hebrew, pastures, or fields of grass, for grassy and rich grounds. Some, instead of translating the word נאות, neoth, which we have rendered pastures, render it shepherds' cots or lodges. If this translation is considered preferable, the meaning of the Psalmist will be, that sheep-cots were prepared in rich pasture grounds, under which he might be protected from the heat of the sun. If even in cold countries the immoderate heat which sometimes occurs is troublesome to a flock of sheep, how could they bear the heat of the summer in Judea, a warm region, without sheepfolds? The verb רבץ, rabats, to lie down, or repose, seems to have a reference to the same thing.

2.2 David has used the phrase, the quiet waters, to express gently flowing waters; for rapid streams are inconvenient for sheep to drink in, and are also for the most part hurtful.

2.3 In this verse, and in the verses following, he explains the last clause of the first verse, I shall not want. He relates how abundantly God had provided for all his necessities, and he does this without departing from the comparison which he employed at the commencement. The amount of what is stated is, that the heavenly Shepherd had omitted nothing which might contribute to make him live happily under his care.

2.4 He, therefore, compares the great abundance of all things requisite for the purposes of the present life which he enjoyed, to meadows richly covered with grass, and to gently flowing streams of water; or he compares the benefit or advantage of such things to sheep-cots; for it would not have been enough to have been fed and satisfied in rich pasture, had there not also been provided waters to drink, and the shadow of the sheep-cot to cool and refresh him.

Verse 3

3.1 He restoreth my soul. As it is the duty of a good shepherd to cherish his sheep, and when they are diseased or weak to nurse and support them, David declares that this was the manner in which he was treated by God. The restoring of the soul, as we have translated it, or the conversion of the soul, as it is, literally rendered, is of the same import as to make anew, or to recover, as has been already stated in the 19 psalm, at the seventh verse.

3.2 By the paths of righteousness, he means easy and plain paths. As he still continues his metaphor, it would be out of place to understand this as referring to the direction of the Holy Spirit. He has stated a little before that God liberally supplies

SCHEDULE A: JOHN CALVIN'S COMMENTARY ON PSALM 23

him with all that is requisite for the maintenance of the present life, and now he adds, that he is defended by him from all trouble. The amount of what is said is, that God is in no respect wanting to his people, seeing he sustains them by his power, invigorates and quickens them, and averts from them whatever is hurtful, that they may walk at ease in plain and straight paths.

3.3 That, however, he may not ascribe anything to his own worth or merit, David represents the goodness of God as the cause of so great liberality, declaring that God bestows all these things upon him for his own name's sake. And certainly his choosing us to be his sheep, and his performing towards us all the offices of a shepherd, is a blessing which proceeds entirely from his free and sovereign goodness, as we shall see in the sixty-fifth psalm.

Verse 4

4.1 Though I should walk. True believers, although they dwell safely under the protection of God, are, notwithstanding, exposed to many dangers, or rather they are liable to all the afflictions which befall mankind in common, that they may the better feel how much they need the protection of God.

4.2 David, therefore, here expressly declares, that if any adversity should befall him, he would lean upon the providence of God. Thus he does not promise himself continual pleasures; but he fortifies himself by the help of God courageously to endure the various calamities with which he might be visited. Pursuing his metaphor, he compares the care which God takes in governing true believers to a shepherd's staff and crook, declaring that he is satisfied with this as all-sufficient for the protection of his life. As a sheep, when it wanders up and down through a dark valley, is preserved safe from the attacks of wild beasts and from harm in other ways, by the presence of the shepherd alone, so David now declares that as often as he shall be exposed to any danger, he will have sufficient defense and protection in being under the pastoral care of God.

4.3 We thus see how, in his prosperity, he never forgot that he was a man, but even then seasonably meditated on the adversities which afterwards might come upon him. And certainly, the reason why we are so terrified, when it pleases God to exercise us with the cross, is, because every man, that he may sleep soundly and undisturbed, wraps himself up in carnal security. But there is a great difference between this sleep of stupidity and the repose which faith produces.

4.4 Since God tries faith by adversity, it follows that no one truly confides in God, but he who is armed with invincible constancy for resisting all the fears with which he may be assailed. Yet David did not mean to say that he was devoid of all fear, but only that he would surmount it so as to go without fear wherever his shepherd should lead him. This appears more clearly from the context. He says, in the first place, I will fear no evil; but immediately adding the reason of this, he openly acknowledges that he seeks a remedy against his fear in contemplating, and having his eyes fixed on, the staff of his shepherd: For thy staff and thy crook comfort me. What need would he have had of that consolation, if he had not been disquieted and agitated with fear? It ought, therefore, to be kept in mind, that when David reflected on the adversities which might befall him, he became victorious over fear and temptations, in no other way than by casting himself on the protection of God. This he had also stated before, although a little more obscurely, in these words, For thou art with me. This implies that he had been afflicted with fear. Had not this been the case, for what purpose could he desire the presence of God?

4.5 Besides, it is not against the common and ordinary calamities of life only that he opposes the protection of God, but against those which distract and confound the minds of men with the darkness of death. For the Jewish grammarians think that צלמות, tsalmaveth, which we have translated the shadow of death, is a compound word, as if one should say deadly shade. David here makes an allusion to the dark recesses or dens of wild beasts, to which when an individual approaches he is suddenly seized at his first entrance with an apprehension and fear of death. Now, since God, in the person of his only begotten Son, has exhibited himself to us as our shepherd, much more clearly than he did in old time to the fathers who lived under the Law, we do not render sufficient honour to his protecting care, if we do not lift our eyes to behold it, and keeping them fixed upon it, tread all fears and terrors under our feet.

Verse 5

5.1 Thou wilt prepare. These words, which are put in the future tense, here denote a continued act. David, therefore, now repeats, without a figure, what he has hitherto declared, concerning the beneficence of God, under the similitude of a shepherd. He tells us that by his liberality he is supplied with all that is necessary for the maintenance of this life. When he says, Thou preparest a table before me, he means that God furnished him with sustenance without trouble or difficulty on his part, just as if a father should stretch forth his hand to give food to his child.

5.2 He enhances this benefit from the additional consideration, that although many malicious persons envy his happiness, and desire his ruin, yea, endeavor to defraud him of the blessing of God; yet God does not desist from showing himself liberal towards him, and from doing him good.

5.3 What he subjoins concerning oil, has a reference to a custom which then prevailed. We know that in old time, ointments were used at the more magnificent feasts, and no man thought he had honourably received his guests if he had not perfumed them therewith. Now, this exuberant store of oil, and also this overflowing cup, ought to be explained as denoting the abundance which goes beyond the mere supply of the common necessaries of life; for it is spoken in commendation of the royal wealth with which, as the sacred historian records, David had been amply furnished.

5.4 All men, it is true, are not treated with the same liberality with which David was treated; but there is not an individual who is not under obligation to God by the benefits which God has conferred upon him, so that we are constrained to acknowledge that he is a kind and liberal Father to all his people. In the meantime, let each of us stir up himself to gratitude to God for his benefits, and the more abundantly these have been bestowed upon us, our gratitude ought to be the greater. If he is ungrateful who, having only a coarse loaf, does not acknowledge in that the fatherly providence of God, how much less can the stupidity of those be tolerated, who glut themselves with the great abundance of the good things of God which they possess, without having any sense or taste of his goodness towards them? David, therefore, by his own example, admonishes the rich of their duty, that they may be the more ardent in the expression of their gratitude to God, the more delicately he feeds them.

5.5 Farther, let us remember, that those who have greater abundance than others are bound to observe moderation not less than if they had only as much of the good things of this life as would serve for their limited and temperate enjoyment. We are too much inclined by nature to excess; and, therefore, when

SCHEDULE A: JOHN CALVIN'S COMMENTARY ON PSALM 23

God is, in respect of worldly things, bountiful to his people, it is not to stir up and nourish in them this disease. All men ought to attend to the rule of Paul, which is laid down in Philippians 4:12, that they "may know both how to be abased, and how to abound." That want may not sink us into despondency, we need to be sustained by patient endurance; and, on the other hand, that too great abundance may not elate us above measure, we need to be restrained by the bridle of temperance. Accordingly, the Lord, when he enriches his own people, restrains, at the same time, the licentious desires of the flesh by the spirit of confidence, so that, of their own accord, they prescribe to themselves rules of temperance.

5.6 Not that it is unlawful for rich men to enjoy more freely the abundance which they possess than if God had given them a smaller portion; but all men ought to beware, (and much more kings,) lest they should be dissolved in voluptuous pleasures. David, no doubt, as was perfectly lawful, allowed himself larger scope than if he had been only one of the common people, or than if he had still dwelt in his father's cottage, but he so regulated himself in the midst of his delicacies, as not at all to take pleasure in stuffing and fattening the body. He knew well how to distinguish between the table which God had prepared for him and a trough for swine.

5.7 It is also worthy of particular notice, that although David lived upon his own lands, the tribute money and other revenues of the kingdom, he gave thanks to God just as if God had daily given him his food with his own hand. From this we conclude that he was not blinded with his riches, but always looked upon God as his householder, who brought forth meat and drink from his own store, and distributed it to him at the proper season.

Verse 6

6.1 **Surely goodness and mercy.** Having recounted the blessings which God had bestowed upon him, he now expresses his undoubted persuasion of the continuance of them to the end of his life. But whence proceeded this confidence, by which he assures himself that the beneficence and mercy of God will accompany him for ever, if it did not arise from the promise by which God is accustomed to season the blessings which he bestows upon true believers, that they may not inconsiderately devour them without having any taste or relish for them?

6.2 When he said to himself before, that even amidst the darkness of death he would keep his eyes fixed in beholding the providence of God, he sufficiently testified that he did not depend upon outward things, nor measured the grace of God according to the judgement of the flesh, but that even when assistance from every earthly quarter failed him, his faith continued shut up in the word of God. Although, therefore, experience led him to hope well, yet it was principally on the promise by which God confirms his people with respect to the future that he depended.

6.3 If it is objected that it is presumption for a man to promise himself a continued course of prosperity in this uncertain and changing world, I answer, that David did not speak in this manner with the view of imposing on God a law; but he hoped for such exercise of God's beneficence towards him as the condition of this world permits, with which he would be contented. He does not say, My cup shall be always full, or, My head shall be always perfumed with oil; but in general he entertains the hope that as the goodness of God never fails, he will be favorable towards him even to the end.

6.4 **I will dwell in the house of Jehovah.** By this concluding sentence he manifestly shows that he does not confine his thoughts to earthly pleasures or comforts; but that the mark at which he aims is fixed in heaven, and to reach this was his great object in all things. It is as if he had said, I do not live for the mere purpose of living, but rather to exercise myself in the fear and service of God, and to make progress daily in all the branches of true godliness. He makes a manifest distinction between himself and ungodly men, who take pleasure only in filling their bellies with luxuriant fare.

6.5 And not only so, but he also intimates that to live to God is, in his estimation, of so great importance, that he valued all the comforts of the flesh only in proportion as they served to enable him to live to God. He plainly affirms, that the end which he contemplated in all the benefits which God had conferred upon him was, that he might dwell in the house of the Lord. Whence it follows, that when deprived of the enjoyment of this blessing, he made no account of all other things; as if he had said, I would take no pleasure in earthly comforts, unless I at the same time belonged to the flock of God, as he also writes in another place, "Happy is that people that is in such a case: yea, happy is that people whose God is the Lord," (Psalms 144:15).

6.6 Why did he desire so greatly to frequent the temple, but to offer sacrifices there along with his fellow-worshippers, and to improve by the other exercises of religion in meditation upon the celestial life? It is, therefore, certain that the mind of David, by the aid of the temporal prosperity which he enjoyed, was elevated to the hope of the everlasting inheritance. From this we conclude, that those men are brutish who propose to themselves any other felicity than that which arises from drawing near to God.

~~~~~~~

Notes on Calvin's commentary:

If the word of God is removed from Psalm 23 as the saints' food and pasture, something must replace it. First Calvin speculated that "pasture" – or rather, the plural "pastures" – might not be the meaning of the Hebrew. Instead, he suggested that the meaning might be "shepherd's lodges" or "sheep-cots," which provide not food but shelter for the shepherds – or, perhaps, for the sheep (2.1). Turning "pasture" to the plural made a singular reference to God's word impossible, and then, by referring the Hebrew to a non-food item, Calvin drove another stake into the traditional doctrine. His uncertain speculations served to undermine the foundation of the traditional doctrine, so that new doctrine could be erected upon it.

However uncertain Calvin was about the appropriateness of the translation "pasture," he was very certain concerning the place and value of worldly benefits, pleasures, and delicacies as the food by which God "allures" and "feeds" his sheep (1.1, 5.4). These crass teachings were befogged with volumes of fair and pious words about humility and the service of God, proving true not only Paul's warning that the false apostles know how to fashion themselves as ministers of righteousness (2Co. 11:15), but also Luther's statement that lies require much babble. Finally, Calvin made David out to be a model, not for lovers of God's word, but for rich men who live in luxury. He presented David as a model for the proper use and enjoyment of, and gratitude for, worldly foods – being the foods of (as he himself enumerated them in his commentary) prosperity, sovereign and great power, the splendour of riches and honours, applause on every side, greatest abundance of temporal good things, princely pleasures, delicacies, comforts, luxuriant fare, and royal wealth (1.2, 1.3, etc.). Meanwhile, he said, the common people should be grateful for their coarse loaf (5.4). Thus was Psalm 23 not written for all, but for kings and the wealthy, and thus did Calvin make their riches and honours to be the pasture of rich saints.

Calvin offered a modified kind of monastic approach to worldly and material things, in that he was intensely focussed on them and upon developing a pious attitude toward them. However, instead of the monkish piety of self-denial and asceticism, he offered the piety of "bridling licentious desires" (5.5) and a controlled "relish" (6.1). Instead of a rule of poverty he prescribed a rule of temperance (5.5), and instead of a holy renunciation of worldly goods, he prescribed a holy gratitude to make riches as ladders to God (1.2).

The notes below, offered in no particular order, provide some final contrasts of Calvin's teaching with that of Coverdale and Luther.

1. As abundantly seen already, Calvin taught here worldly riches alone as David's blessings (5.6, 5.4). However, Coverdale taught that God's word is the real treasure, and the only sure one.

2. Calvin taught that the table set before David in the sight of his enemies was the temporal benefits that God provided him without any trouble or difficulty on his part (5.1). Coverdale wrote that the table set before David in the presence of his enemies is the great and wonderful power of the word of God, and the knowledge of it (p. 48).

3. Calvin taught that David's "exuberant store of oil" and "overflowing cup" referred to his excess of worldly goods above the necessaries of life, which excess he said David commended (5.3). Coverdale wrote that the oil in Psalm 23 signifies joy and gladness, and the cup is the rich comfort of the word of God (p. 52).

4. Calvin said that David "does not say, My cup shall be always full," but he only hoped for such benefits as "the condition of the world permits." (6.3). However, Coverdale knew nothing of such a sad, weak, unchristian hope. He wrote that neither the world, nor trouble, nor death could ever empty the cup that Jesus fills (pp. 54-55). Thus the true cup is always full.

5. As regards death, Calvin stoked a fear of it, comparing it to the "dark recesses of wild beasts" that fill us with fear, and said we do not render sufficient honour to God if we do not tread the fears and terrors under our feet (4.5). Inconceivably for a Christian teacher, he did not mention Christ, nor hold the cross before fearful, dying eyes. He offered not a drop of comfort, but added the burden of an obligation to honour God by treading fears under our feet, apparently by our own strength.

Coverdale, on the other hand, said the consciences of the faithful are "quiet, glad, and at rest in the midst of all temptations and troubles, yea even of death" (p.52). However, he wrote elsewhere that if fears do assail in death, the remedy is to declare Christ to the troubled soul; namely, his cross and death for our salvation, how he will change our lowly bodies to be like his glorious body, and how our life is hid in him. In the *Treatise on Death,* Coverdale wrote that Christ must "be printed into the feeble, troubled, and doubtful consciences of the sick."[1] Also: "In Christ we have a mighty, efficacious image of grace, of life, and of salvation, in such sort that we Christians should fear neither death nor other misfortune."[2] Further, it is Christ who has tread death under his feet for us (Ge. 3:15, 1Co. 15:57).

---

[1] Myles Coverdale, *Treatise on Death* (Canada: Baruch House Publishing, 2021), 55.
[2] Ibid., 72.

SCHEDULE A: NOTES ON CALVIN'S COMMENTARY

Coverdale also warned that to contemplate death without Christ, as Calvin did here, is a fatal error: "When we now behold death and the pangs of death in itself with our own feeble reason, without Christ, without God's word, and especially out of season (that is to say, in the danger of death), then death has its full power and strength in our feeble nature and kills us with the greater pain, so that we forget God and are lost forever."[3]

6. Further stoking fearfulness, Calvin said twice that David meditated on possible adversities that might come upon him, and that by such foreboding meditations he was strengthened and made victorious (4.3, 4.4). However, Coverdale said that it is by knowing and meditating on God's glorious word, and by faith in it, that we are strengthened and made victorious (p.49).

7. The only time Calvin mentioned the cross was to refer it to man's troubles and adversities in this life. He said that God is "pleased" to exercise us with the cross due to our "carnal security" and "sleep of stupidity" (4.3). He never spoke of the comfort that the cross is to man _in_ his adversities, but he only taught the cross _as_ an adversity. This is a pernicious re-emphasis.

8. Calvin said David "confessed himself a poor sheep, that he might have God for his shepherd" (1.5). This is a very ambiguous statement. He also wrote that God had "no less care" of David than a shepherd has of the sheep who are committed to his charge (1.4). These are chary words.

Coverdale said clearly and emphatically that he considered himself rich to have God as his shepherd. Further, God takes *much more* care of his sheep than any other shepherd can or will; he provides "wondrous well" for his sheep (p. 25), and he is "a

---

[3] Ibid., 62-63. Gently updated.

thousand times" more diligent than any good shepherd of this world (p. 28). Such words proceed from a heart of praise.

9. Calvin wrote that our happiness is that God's hand is stretched forth to govern us (1.6). On the other hand, Coverdale wrote that our joy is in the word of God, which quickens the soul inwardly (p. 21).

10. Calvin said that the more "delicately" (luxuriously) God feeds rich men, the more "ardent" their expression of gratitude should be (5.40). This sets the rich above the poor as peculiarly blessed and favoured by God. It also stokes covetousness.

To bring also William Tyndale into this discussion, in his prologue to the book of Numbers he warned that riches and honour may corrupt the mind and draw the heart away from God. Tyndale is known for his saying that "prosperity is a right curse."

11. Calvin, by not mentioning Christ even once in his entire long commentary on Psalm 23, but riches only, invented ladders to God without Christ, as the Jews do. Coverdale, however, mentioned Christ frequently in the *Sweet Exposition*, by whom and only by whom we have the knowledge of God. For no one comes to the Father except by him (Joh. 14:6).

12. Lastly, Calvin's doctrine of riches as the means by which God draws man to him mocks the ministry of the word and gospel. It also opposes the Lord Jesus, who said that it is easier for a camel to go through the eye of a needle than for a rich man to enter into heaven (Mk. 10:25). Further, the necessary inference from Calvin's teaching is that rich men, by their greater abundance, have greater ladders to God than the poor. This is plainly offensive to grace, truth, mercy, and the gospel. Indeed, it is another gospel.

Glossary

This glossary gives words and phrases that are likely to cause difficulty to modern readers. Within the book, the Parker Society editor also added footnotes defining expressions that were obsolete in the 19th century.

affiance	trust or faith.
again	in return (back again).
approved of God	proven, shown, or attested by God.
away with(al)	put up with or get along with.
bewray, verb	to divulge secrets; to discredit a person by exposing his secrets or sins; more generally, to reveal, make known, show.
captain	leader.
certify (someone)	make (a person) certain or sure (*of* a matter); to assure, inform certainly.
Christ his sheep	Christ's sheep.
church militant	members of Christ who are yet living in this earth and doing battle with the world, the flesh, and the devil pursuant to their baptismal vows (as opposed to those who have died and are now at rest).
comfort, verb	The old meaning included strengthening a person's spirit or resolve as well as providing solace.
comfortable	able to give comfort, comforting.

commodity	benefit, convenience, advantage, or interest.
conceit	according to the context: notion, opinion, sometimes frame of mind or disposition.
conditions	characteristics.
contentation	willing acceptance.
convenient	befitting, proper.
conversation	life, manner of life, way of living.
crack, verb	boast, sometimes with sense of scorn toward others. Past form 'crake.'
dainty	particular about comfort and luxury.
despise, verb	hate, scorn, or hold in contempt; more weakly, neglect or ignore.
despite	contemptuous and injurious attitude or action.
dizzard	idiotic; as a noun, idiot.
doctrine	in some contexts, a lesson or piece of instruction.
dubitation	uncertainty, hesitation.
Easter	Passover. See also 'passah.'
entreating	treatment.
fain	in "would fain": would gladly, would like to.
fly, verb	flee, escape away.
force not	care not, have no concern for.
froward	habitually contrary, rebellious. More generally, evilly inclined.
fumishness	irascibility, inclination to fume.
furnish, verb	supply, provide, prepare; sometimes, adorn.

gear	according to the context: (1) doctrine; in depreciatory sense, stuff and nonsense (2) apparatus, equipment (3) armour, arms (see also 'harness' and 'ordnance').
ghostly	spiritual or spiritually.
godly	divine, as in "godly power" or "godly wisdom."
hale, verb	pull, drag.
happen of course	happen as a matter of course.
harness	defensive armour or equipment, military accoutrement. See also 'ordnance' and 'gear.'
health	salvation.
Helias	Elijah.
Hierusalem	Jerusalem.
holiday	holy day.
honesty	decency, whence *honest* or decent.
hucker mucker	secretly, secretively.
hurley-burlies	commotions, tumults, uproars.
inconvenience	according to the context: disagreement or strife; sometimes, absurdity.
indurate	hardened.
Jewry (also spelled Jury)	depending on the context, Judea in ancient Rome, or more generally Israel or Judah; also, the Jewish people collectively.
keep, verb	guard, protect, watch over.
lovers	loving friends.
lust, noun or verb	wish or desire.

lusty, lustily	according to the context: willing, strong, valiant, vigorous, desirous. Also pleasing (as in "lusty to the eyes"). Whence *lustily*: willingly, valiantly, etc.
meat	food, sustenance.
meddle (with), verb	to concern or occupy oneself with or in a matter. The sense of undue interference was not always present in older use.
naughty	according to the context: worthless, morally bad, or blameworthy.
noise, verb	tell widely as a report or rumour.
noisome	harmful, noxious; more weakly, annoying.
notify (to), verb	tell, inform.
nurture	upbringing or education.
open, verb	according to the context: declare, reveal, disclose, or show.
ordnance	armour, weapons, and military supplies. See also 'harness' and 'gear.'
original	origin, fount, or source.
passah	Passover. See also 'Easter.'
pelf	rubbish, frippery. Also riches; in depreciative sense, ill-gotten goods or riches as a corrupting influence.
prevent, verb	go before.
prince	high ruler.
publish, verb	declare widely, make known abroad.
save, verb	in some contexts, safeguard.

GLOSSARY

scholars	students.
science	knowledge; also a field of study.
sentence	judgement or meaning.
shifting	wily maneuvering.
stomach	used like 'heart' or 'breast' to indicate the inward seat of emotion, feelings, or secret thoughts.
sweep-stake	in "make sweep-stake": remove totally; i.e., sweep away.
target	a shield or buckler to ward off blows.
tell, verb	count (past form 'told' = counted).
temptation(s)	in some contexts, trial(s).
token	sign.
trow, verb	trust, believe. In "I trow (you)" = I trust, suppose, think, believe.
trusty	depending on the context, either trustworthy or trusting.
tutor	guardian, protector.
ugsome	horrible, loathsome.
unspeakable, unoutspeakable	indescribable, inexpressible, unutterable.
utter, verb	reveal by deed or declare by word.
wealth	well-being, welfare.
Whitsunday	Pentecost.
witty	wise or prudent.
wot, verb	know.
wroth	deep anger or resentment.

www.ingramcontent.com/pod-product-compliance
Lightning Source LLC
Chambersburg PA
CBHW020905080526
44589CB00011B/451